Our Daily Bread

BIBLE

WORD SEARCH
& ACTIVITY BOOK

VOL. 2

Our Daily Bread
Publishing™

Our Daily Bread Bible Word Search and Activity Book, Volume 2
© 2022 by Our Daily Bread Publishing

Cover and Interior design by InsideOut Creative Arts, Inc.

ISBN: 978-1-64070-168-7

Printed in the United States of America

22 23 24 25 26 27 28 29 / 8 7 6 5 4 3 2 1

LESSER-KNOWN WOMEN OF THE BIBLE WORD SEARCH

Words may be horizontal, vertical, or diagonal, forward or backward, and may overlap.

```
R P C N Q F Y R T Y V Q C S R V
O E E E A T F S A Y X V O H A L
V N R X S A D O M R Q G F V H O
Z I T S L P M H A Z S X D N I I
I N A P C W S A R I I P S T N S
J N Z B R F J E H K U B Y F O Y
M A T E I R I W K Q Q N N P A Z
U H D A Z G N A S E N A T H M E
L T H J L C A N D A C E Y C B G
Y U E F O R A I S R S B C X I L
V A A K S A H T L V T J H W L A
P E R S I S N U P F M G E D H H
E L H R C Y V N F G J K P K A E
H I S A L O M E A O X P J U H O
J X S S U S A N N A R N E M V G
C O R P A H E S V A S H T I L K
```

ABIGAIL	EGLAH	PENINNAH	TAMAR
AKSAH	JOANNA	PERSIS	VASHTI
AHINOAM	LOIS	SALOME	
ASENATH	NAAMAH	SUSANNA	
BILHAH	ORPAH	SYNTYCHE	

—— *Answer key on page 114.* ——

LANDS OF THE BIBLE

Match the town to the description.

A. BEERSHEBA   F. CAPERNAUM
B. BETHLEHEM   G. EPHESUS
C. BETHSAIDA   H. JERUSALEM
D. CAESAREA   I. JOPPA
E. CAESAREA PHILIPPI J. LAODICEA

____ 1. In this city, Paul's messages led to a riot because the Artemis shrine makers said Paul was hurting their business.

____ 2. This was the hometown of Peter, Philip, and Andrew.

____ 3. When David's commander Joab attacked this city, he entered it through its water source.

____ 4. This town, named after a Roman leader, was where Peter met the centurion Cornelius.

____ 5. According to Genesis 26:23–25, Isaac built an altar in this town.

____ 6. When Jonah left for Tarshish, he got on a boat in this city.

____ 7. When Jesus asked the disciples, "Who do people say I am?" they were at the foot of Mount Herman at this town.

____ 8. In Micah 5:2, this town was described as "small among the clans of Judah," but out of it would come "one who will be ruler over Israel."

____ 9. In Revelation 3, Jesus called the people of this city "lukewarm."

____ 10. According to Matthew 4:13–14, Jesus lived in this town after he left His hometown of Nazareth.

——— Answer key on page 114. ———

PAUL SAID IT IN 1 CORINTHIANS

*Complete the apostle Paul's quotes by
supplying the missing word.*

1. "The message of the cross is _____ to
those who are perishing" (1 Corinthians 1:18).

2. "I resolved to know nothing while I was with you except
Jesus Christ and him _____" (1 Corinthians 2:2).

3. "Don't you know that you yourselves are God's
_____ and that God's Spirit lives in [you]?"
(1 Corinthians 3:16).

4. "Love does not delight in evil but rejoices with the
_____. It always protects, always trusts,
always hopes, always perseveres" (1 Corinthians 13:6–7).

5. "These three remain: faith, hope and love. But the greatest of these is _____" (1 Corinthians 13:13).

6. "_____ has been swallowed up in victory"
(1 Corinthians 15:54).

7. "When I became a man, I put aside _____
things" (1 Corinthians 13:11 CSB).

8. "I planted the seed, Apollos watered it, but God has
been making it _____" (1 Corinthians 3:6).

9. "Let the one who boasts boast in the
_____" (1 Corinthians 1:31).

10. "Christ did not send me to _____, but to
preach the gospel" (1 Corinthians 1:17).

—— *Answer key on page 114.* ——

THE PEOPLE OF MATTHEW'S GENEALOGY
WORD SEARCH

Words may be horizontal, vertical, or diagonal, forward or backward, and may overlap.

```
T B I B W C X J O S I A H P P U
A B R A H A M U R U E A G E V F U
M U P S A R J E B T F S A R L H E
A S U J O P W J C Q M Y W E O N W
T O A Z H L F D K X A F E Z M Q H
T Y B M Z R O F B A N V T Y O W E
H Y C E M I G M G A A F C A B J E
A P X F D I A T O X S S D I V O J
N G X F N D N H Z N S N E J L S U
Y T W Q Q Y O A R T E N N H E E D
W N J J U V O R D Q H X X I B P A
H E Z E K I A H S A L M O N U H H
D R W S J W K K X J B G J X D E N
L W W S R P O Z C L L B O A Z L P
X Q V E F I I V J P T O F Q D E V
L J A C O B Q V E L E A Z A R W H
P D A V I D O Z S C I S A A C G X
```

ABRAHAM	HEZEKIAH	JOSIAH	PEREZ
AMMINADAB	ISAAC	JUDAH	SALMON
BOAZ	JACOB	MANASSEH	SOLOMON
DAVID	JESSE	MATTHAN	UZZIAH
ELEAZAR	JOSEPH	OBED	

PROVERBS 1-4
WORD SEARCH

Words may be horizontal, vertical, or diagonal,
forward or backward, and may overlap.

```
P  V  D  P  U  T  X  H  U  M  B  L  E  K  F
D  I  S  C  E  R  N  I  N  G  I  J  C  Q  A
A  C  Z  B  K  V  H  T  L  D  B  W  P  U  I
D  O  P  L  P  R  D  T  C  O  W  B  R  B  T
D  M  R  E  R  K  I  W  L  U  V  T  E  L  H
T  M  U  S  O  G  N  G  U  A  N  E  C  A  F
E  A  D  S  S  R  H  O  H  M  E  E  I  M  U
A  N  E  E  P  A  T  G  W  T  L  H  O  E  L
C  D  N  D  E  C  M  N  N  L  E  A  U  L  N
H  S  T  F  R  E  T  O  A  O  E  O  S  E  E
I  U  P  R  I  G  H  T  D  S  M  D  U  S  S
N  T  D  Z  T  R  W  B  D  S  A  O  G  S  S
G  W  E  Q  Y  N  M  W  Y  Z  I  E  L  E  K
U  K  X  Q  H  O  N  O  R  D  P  W  L  O  P
A  D  I  S  C  R  E  T  I  O  N  C  N  P  S
```

BLAMELESS	HONOR	RIGHTEOUS
BLESSED	HUMBLE	SOLOMON
COMMANDS	KNOWLEDGE	TEACHING
DISCERNING	LOVE	UPRIGHT
DISCRETION	PLEASANT	WISDOM
FAITHFULNESS	PRECIOUS	
GRACE	PROSPERITY	
HEALTH	PRUDENT	

—— *Answer key on page 115.* ——

CREATION STORY FILL-IN

Complete the following verses from the creation story.

1. "Now the earth was _____ and
   _____, darkness was over the surface of
   the deep" (v. 2).

2. "God saw that the light was good, and he separated the
   _____ from the _____" (v. 4).

3. "God called the vault '_____'" (v. 8).

4. "And God said, 'Let the water under the sky be gathered to one place, and let _____
   _____ appear'" (v. 9). 'd'

5. "God called the dry ground '_____,' and the
   gathered waters he called '_____'" (v. 10).

6. "The land produced vegetation: plants bearing
   _____ . . . according to their _____" (v. 12).

7. "God made two great lights—the greater light to
   govern the _____ and the lesser light to
   govern the _____" (v. 16).

8. "God . . . said to them, 'Be _____ and
   increase in _____'" (v. 28).

—— *Answer key on page 115.* ——

PEOPLE GROUPS
WORD SEARCH

Words may be horizontal, vertical, or diagonal,
forward or backward, and may overlap.

```
I  B  H  R  V  R  A  M  O  R  I  T  E  S  O  W
A  E  A  E  N  H  J  X  Y  H  H  A  W  Q  F  A
Z  A  D  B  B  A  U  A  J  N  I  M  X  G  P  P
Y  G  S  O  Y  R  P  Z  V  L  T  M  G  R  A  I
E  V  G  S  M  L  E  C  R  Q  T  O  P  E  O  S
G  G  O  F  Y  I  O  W  U  A  I  N  T  E  W  R
N  O  Y  M  P  R  T  N  S  X  T  I  G  K  S  A
I  W  Z  P  O  I  I  E  I  X  E  T  A  S  O  E
Z  M  M  Z  T  A  Z  A  S  A  S  E  L  B  J  L
I  I  L  Z  J  I  B  J  N  H  N  S  I  F  U  I
R  O  M  A  N  S  A  I  S  S  A  S  L  P  D  T
J  Y  Z  J  S  X  Z  N  T  R  N  F  E  A  E  E
Q  M  M  X  Q  E  M  J  S  E  B  I  A  D  A  S
Z  S  A  M  A  R  I  T  A  N  S  L  N  C  N  R
P  H  I  L  I  S  T  I  N  E  S  C  S  Q  S  L
B  P  E  R  S  I  A  N  S  M  O  F  X  C  N  L
```

AMMONITES	GALILEANS	MOABITES
AMORITES	GREEKS	PERSIANS
ASSYRIANS	HEBREWS	PHILISTINES
BABYLONIANS	HITTITES	ROMANS
EDOMITES	ISRAELITES	SAMARITANS
EGYPTIANS	JUDEANS	

SHAKESPEARE OR THE BIBLE?

*One of the quotes for each number is from
William Shakespeare; the other is from the Bible.
Select the one from the Bible.*

____ 1. a. "The better part of valor is discretion."
   b. "The total number of chief officers of the mighty men of valor was two thousand six hundred."

____ 2. a. "Love looks not with the eyes, but with the mind."
   b. "Many waters cannot quench love, neither can floods drown it."

____ 3. a. "A time to be born, and a time to die; a time to plant, and a time to pluck up what is planted."
   b. "The valiant never taste of death but once."

____ 4. a. "A man can die but once."
   b. "Man is like a breath; his days are like a passing shadow."

____ 5. a. "A man without self-control is like a city broken into and left without walls."
   b. "To thine own self be true."

____ 6. a. "The evil that men do lives after them; The good is oft interrèd with their bones."
   b. "Woe to those who call evil good and good evil."

_____ 7. a. "The rich rules over the poor, and the borrower is the slave of the lender."

b. "Neither a borrower nor a lender be; for loan oft loses both itself and friend, and borrowing dulls the edge of husbandry."

_____ 8. a. "I am a man more sinned against than sinning."

b. "Whoever conceals his transgressions will not prosper."

_____ 9. a. "Now is the winter of our discontent."

b. "The lazy man will not plow because of winter; He will beg during harvest and have nothing."

_____ 10. a. "How much better to get wisdom than gold!"

b. "All that glitters is not gold."

———— Answer key on page 116. ————

HEALINGS BY JESUS

Provide the answers for these events.

1. Jesus healed the servant of this military leader.

2. At Capernaum Jesus healed this person's mother-in-law.

3. This man's daughter was raised from the dead.

4. Jesus healed this blind man at Jericho.

5. This person was healed after Peter cut off his ear.

6. This person touched Jesus's robe and was healed.

7. Jesus healed this disease when He "reached out and touched the man" then told him not to tell anyone about it except the priest.

8. Jesus healed this withered body part in the synagogue on the Sabbath.

9. What was the marital status of the woman whose son Jesus raised in Nain?

10. The paralyzed man in Bethseda was trying to get into this to be healed before Jesus came and healed him.

——— *Answer key on page 116.* ———

COMMON NOUNS IN GENESIS
WORD SEARCH

*Words may be horizontal, vertical, or diagonal,
forward or backward, and may overlap.*

```
Z F P I L L A R H Y I M C Y M
B L S O C K E T E I U N U Q B
W O M V Q O H Z A S B U P D I
O O U L I B V P V K E H B R R
N D P K O R L E E B G H E E T
E R S U Y F T E N P I U A A H
S E R P E N T D S A N D R M R
M A G S Y A U Y B S N A E S I
S C R E A T U R E S I T R Q G
T R A L T A R W D D N N X T H
U A A C O F F I N L G O G N T
E Y M V S T A I R W A Y N S S
U T O W E R T B C A M E L S C
D E S C E N D A N T S F V H R
P Y B G T E L U F A M I N E C
```

ALTAR	CREATURES	PILLAR
BEGINNING	CUPBEARER	RAVEN
BIRTHRIGHT	DESCENDANTS	SERPENT
BLESSING	DREAMS	STAIRWAY
CAMELS	FAMINE	SOCKET
COFFIN	FLOOD	TOWER
COVENANT	HEAVENS	

SOLOMON'S TEMPLE
WORD SEARCH

*Words may be horizontal, vertical, or diagonal,
forward or backward, and may overlap.*

```
P  X  I  S  T  O  N  E  C  U  T  T  E  R  S  C
L  O  P  A  C  C  G  O  L  D  V  B  T  Y  I  A
E  L  O  X  E  F  N  B  R  S  V  O  O  S  S  B
B  I  R  V  Q  S  D  K  H  S  K  G  E  J  P  R
A  V  T  F  M  J  A  H  G  C  N  I  S  V  Q  O
N  E  I  E  C  N  V  L  S  N  E  I  T  P  N  N
O  C  C  Y  N  L  N  N  T  L  I  D  S  R  A  Z
N  C  O  I  R  I  S  O  E  A  A  L  A  A  R  E
C  N  H  U  P  O  P  G  I  K  R  T  E  R  B  J
U  K  I  E  R  I  T  S  N  T  B  M  I  N  S  H
B  A  R  P  R  T  L  S  T  I  A  J  A  P  A  L
I  O  O  A  S  U  Y  L  E  O  V  D  I  R  A  P
T  H  D  K  E  L  B  A  A  R  N  R  N  C  I  C
S  I  D  F  G  F  Q  I  R  R  E  E  A  U  L  H
Z  T  A  K  Z  E  O  X  M  D  S  L  E  C  O  Y
L  A  M  P  S  T  A  N  D  S  C  B  C  V  R  F
```

ALTAR	CLERESTORY	PANELING
ARK	COURTYARD	PILLARS
BASINS	CUBITS	PINE
BRONZE	FOUNDATION	PORTICO
CAPITALS	GOLD	SEA
CARVINGS	LAMPSTANDS	STONECUTTERS
CEDARS	LEBANON	
CHERUBIM	OLIVE	

Note: These words are from various Bible translations, as well as
the original Hebrew and Greek.

JESUS QUOTE FILL-IN

Fill in the blank.

1. "Do not think that I have come to _____ the Law or the Prophets; . . . but to _____ them" (Matthew 5:17).

2. "Whoever does the will of my Father in heaven is my brother and sister and _____" (Matthew 12:50).

3. "If someone forces you to go one mile, go with him _____ miles" (Matthew 5:41).

4. "No one can serve two _____, for either he will hate the one and love the other, or he will be devoted to the one and despise the other. You cannot serve God and money" (Matthew 6:24 ESV).

5. "Everyone who hears these words of mine and puts them into practice is like a _____ man who built his house on the _____" (Matthew 7:24).

6. "Do not put the Lord your God to the _____" Luke 4:12.

7. "_____, for the kingdom of heaven has come near" (Matthew 4:17).

8. "Very truly I tell you, no one can see the kingdom of God unless they are _____ _____" (John 3:3).

9. "Whoever drinks the water I give them will never _____" (John 4:14).

10. "The work of God is this: to _____ in the one he has sent" (John 6:29).

—— *Answer key on page 117.* ——

NAMES OF GOD
WORD SEARCH

*Words may be horizontal, vertical, or diagonal,
forward or backward, and may overlap.*

```
D A Y S P R I N G P O C A O A
E D A Y S T A R L L G O D G L
B L P P K I N G P U Z R O C P
R O O E U U L Y R T A N N R H
I C J R A X O S X R D E A E A
D O Y E D B G J G U V R I A I
E M Q A H K O B B T O S M T M
G F B U H O S Q R H C T A O M
R O H N S W V X P A A O J R A
O R A C L J E A R G T N E D N
O T U B B A K H H H E E S P U
M E K B B S A L M I G H T Y E
Y R Z I F A T H E R T B Y K L
X D E L I V E R E R Z K B P H
K S R A R E D E E M E R M X R
```

ABBA
ADONAI
ADVOCATE
ALMIGHTY
ALPHA
BRIDEGROOM
COMFORTER
CORNERSTONE

CREATOR
DAYSPRING
DAYSTAR
DELIVERER
FATHER
IMMANUEL
JEHOVAH
KING

LOGOS
LORD
MAJESTY
REDEEMER
TRUTH
YAHWEH

ANIMAL TERMS IN JOB 39
WORD SEARCH

*Words may be horizontal, vertical, or diagonal,
forward or backward, and may overlap.*

```
M F F U R R O W D T F N T Y B
K F B Y K W K Z D F L G V U I
F S D E J I M X O D M O U N R
R E H Z Z N J O N V Y A F A T
P F A A B G J I K I A T A H H
Q I Z T W S X Y E E D S W O D
Z K N D H K A X Y X G H N R C
Y O P I J E H A D O E G B S N
H N A B O P R M S C O Y S E E
Y E W K U N Y S X Q R M E O S
N W S F X O S R V O J S A E T
Z J P H A R N E S S N O G Q W
O S T R I C H D T G C A L T S
J A V Z S T O R K T C R E U H
M F L I G H T M A N E B Q W A
```

BIRTH	FEATHERS	HORSE	STORK
DOE	FLIGHT	MANE	WINGS
DONKEY	FURROW	NEST	
EAGLE	GOATS	OSTRICH	
EGGS	HARNESS	PAWS	
FAWN	HAWK	SOAR	

WHICH IS IT? ELISHA, ELIJAH, OR BOTH?

*Determine whether Elisha, Elijah, or both
are being described.*

A. ELISHA   B. ELIJAH   C. BOTH

____ 1. Comes first in the Bible story.

____ 2. Part of the "school of prophets."

____ 3. Left a letter of warning for King Jehoram.

____ 4. Confronted the gods on Mount Carmel.

____ 5. Was fed by ravens at the Brook Kerith.

____ 6. Turned bad water into clean water.

____ 7. Raised a boy from the dead.

____ 8. Called down fire from heaven to kill fifty soldiers.

____ 9. Fled from Queen Jezebel in fear.

____ 10. Filled a widow's jars with oil.

____ 11. Picked up the other's mantle and used it miraculously.

____ 12. Crossed the Jordan on dry land.

FLYING CREATURES IN THE BIBLE
WORD SEARCH

Words may be horizontal, vertical, or diagonal, forward or backward, and may overlap.

```
F  L  E  J  B  O  E  G  O  X  J  H  S  H  F
P  A  R  T  R  I  D  G  E  W  V  E  X  D  U
K  B  K  K  H  N  V  L  L  W  U  R  B  O  M
A  W  I  F  D  E  Z  E  H  M  L  O  X  V  O
T  T  T  L  A  I  H  W  V  X  T  N  C  E  T
Y  R  E  E  M  L  H  O  I  X  U  E  B  R  H
D  L  J  A  U  T  C  S  R  S  R  S  A  N  R
I  Q  U  A  I  L  Y  O  F  N  E  M  T  F  Q
D  I  Y  S  T  O  R  K  N  B  E  P  G  L  H
C  O  R  M  O  R  A  N  T  I  B  T  F  Y  A
R  G  R  A  S  S  H  O  P  P  E  R  V  Y  W
B  F  J  H  D  A  J  A  I  Y  K  J  J  J  K
Y  N  O  Z  O  S  P  R  E  Y  U  A  T  R  E
S  P  I  G  E  O  N  V  K  B  E  E  Z  N  I
S  F  Z  E  J  G  N  A  T  Q  S  O  W  L  T
```

BAT	FLY	KATYDID	PIGEON
BEE	GNAT	KITE	QUAIL
CORMORANT	GRASSHOPPER	MOTH	STORK
DOVE	HAWK	OSPREY	VULTURE
FALCON	HERON	OWL	
FLEA	HORNET	PARTRIDGE	

BIBLE FOOD AND DRINK CROSSWORD

"So whether you eat or drink or whatever you do, do it all for the glory of God." —1 Corinthians 10:31

Across

2. Tree fruit that refreshed the woman in Song of Songs 2.

5. Proverbs 30:33 says churned cream produces this.

7. Wilderness people collected this every morning.

9. Rebekah made a "tasty meal" from this.

11. Nazarites were not allowed to drink wine, grape juice, or this sour liquid.

12. Pan-cooked grain offerings had flour and this oil.

14. Jacob gave it to Esau to eat with bread.

16. Jesus served this liquid at the Last Supper.

17. Israelites seasoned grain offerings with this.

19. The Promised Land flowed with milk and this.

20. Jesus hinted that a dad would not give his son scorpions when the son asked for these.

Down

1. A special treat from God as a break from manna.

3. John ate these with wild honey.

4. Manna was white, like this seed.

5. Abraham asked Sarah to bake it for visitors.

6. This offering is the finest flour (Leviticus 2).

8. David took this dairy product to his brothers' commander.

9. Promised Land fruit carried on poles.

10. The Promised Land flowed with this and honey.

13. Water-borne food Israelites missed after leaving Egypt.

15. Manna taste: this with honey.

18. Mixture of flour and water Israelites took out of Egypt.

PSALM 19
WORD SEARCH

*Words may be horizontal, vertical, or diagonal,
forward or backward, and may overlap.*

```
P  C  I  P  A  O  R  D  I  N  A  N  C  E  S  H
D  P  H  T  K  M  A  W  M  S  P  E  E  C  H  W
R  N  R  A  J  B  D  C  I  R  C  U  I  T  G  O
A  C  E  O  M  K  N  O  W  L  E  D  G  E  C  R
D  X  T  M  C  P  W  M  H  P  Y  H  Z  A  O  K
I  T  X  B  G  L  I  V  O  E  W  V  H  R  M  P
A  C  H  S  K  L  A  O  H  R  A  C  U  J  M  R
N  Y  B  U  D  O  O  I  N  F  D  T  F  G  A  E
T  T  E  N  T  N  L  R  M  E  T  S  D  L  N  C
P  A  V  I  L  I  O  N  Y  C  U  Q  E  V  D  E
G  I  K  E  A  R  T  H  O  T  L  L  C  I  N  P
X  T  R  U  S  T  W  O  R  T  H  Y  N  P  K  T
B  R  I  D  E  G  R  O  O  M  E  B  X  B  O  S
P  S  T  A  T  U  T  E  S  D  Q  S  H  N  B  G
C  F  Q  H  I  D  D  E  N  M  J  Y  I  N  U  J
T  A  H  E  A  V  E  N  S  N  H  M  S  W  Y  S
```

BRIDEGROOM	HIDDEN	SPEECH
CHAMPION	KNOWLEDGE	STATUTES
CIRCUIT	ORDINANCES	SUN
COMMAND	PERFECT	TENT
EARTH	PRECEPTS	TRUSTWORTHY
GLORY	PROCLAIM	WISE
HEAT	RADIANT	WORK
HEAVENS	SKIES	

Note: These terms are from various Bible translations.

I'VE JUST SEEN JESUS:
POST-RESURRECTION APPEARANCES

Provide the answers for
these post-resurrection appearances.

1. The first of Jesus's friends to see Him alive again.

2. The first to reach the tomb and look inside.

3. The second to reach the tomb and look inside.

4. What the disciples thought they saw when Jesus first appeared to them.

5. The town the two disciples were going to when Jesus joined their walk.

6. The disciple who was not with the Twelve when Jesus appeared after passing through locked doors.

7. Jesus showed Thomas this to erase his doubts about Jesus.

8. What Jesus was making for the disciples when they came in from fishing.

9. The largest number of people who saw Jesus at once after the resurrection (according to Bible accounts).

10. This was where Jesus and His followers were when He ascended to heaven.

—— *Answer key on page 120.* ——

MIRACLES IN THE WILDERNESS

Provide the answers for
these miracles that occurred in the wilderness.

1. God allowed the Israelites to cross this body of water on dry land.

2. This man's staff budded.

3. The weather phenomenon that brought quail to the people.

4. Moses went up this mountain to get the Ten Commandments.

5. The metal on the snake pole that the people looked to for healing.

6. This guided the Israelites during the day.

7. This guided the Israelites during the night.

8. The disease that struck Miriam, Moses's sister.

9. This army was lost in the same sea the Israelites crossed.

10. Moses threw this into bitter water to make it sweet.

11. The second time Moses drew water from a rock, he was supposed to do this instead of hitting it.

12. This man was swallowed up by the earth for opposing Moses.

—— *Answer key on page 120.* ——

CHARACTERISTICS OF THE GODLY
WORD SEARCH

Words may be horizontal, vertical, or diagonal, forward or backward, and may overlap.

```
V L P Q Y R B O L D V A V N O
C C U A X G B Q M O K D Y G C
O Y O T T E E G R I E V M O
Y B C M R I O N J Q N V R E M
L E E O P U E B E U D O W R M
I F S D N A T N Z R S U B C I
N A H Y I T S H T P O T Z I T
N I G U E E E S F O O U W F T
O T T P M E N N I U N V S U E
C H S U F B Z T T O L C H L D
E F Q T D I L I G E N T L E M
N U C N A R C E X O W A X T E
T L K B L A M E L E S S T Q E
J K F O R G I V I N G I Q E K
Y P U R E N T A H H O L Y Y Q
```

BLAMELESS	DILIGENT	HUMBLE	OBEDIENT
BOLD	FAITHFUL	INNOCENT	PATIENT
COMMITTED	FORGIVING	JUST	PURE
COMPASSIONATE	GENEROUS	KIND	TRUTHFUL
CONTENT	GENTLE	MEEK	
DEVOUT	HOLY	MERCIFUL	

MOSES CROSSWORD

"Moses was faithful as a servant in all God's house."
—Hebrews 3:5

Across

3. Where Moses settled after fleeing Egypt.

5. The effect on Moses's face from being with God.

6. Moses's crime while in Egypt.

10. Moses's sister.

12. Moses's father-in-law who assisted him.

13. River from which Moses was rescued.

14. Moses's brother and spokesman.

16. Moses's mother saved him by putting him in this.

Down

1. He adopted Moses.

2. Moses's wife.

4. Number of plagues visited on Pharaoh.

5. Accused of speaking "blasphemous words against Moses."

7. Number of books of the Bible Moses wrote.

8. Age of Moses when he returned to Egypt.

9. Years Moses was in exile.

11. Land where Moses was buried.

12. Moses's aide and successor.

15. Moses's job while in exile.

THE ARK OF THE COVENANT

*Provide the answers for these facts about
the ark of the covenant.*

1. What the top of the ark was called

2. The two-dimensional geometric shape of the ark

3. The only right way to carry the ark

4. He died when he touched the ark to prevent it from
   falling over

5. In the wilderness, the ark resided in this structure

6. Where the ark normally stayed after Solomon's time

7. The people group who once took the ark from the
   Israelites

8. When this group had the ark, this happened to its
   people

9. The three things kept inside the ark

10. These angelic creatures were fashioned from gold for
    the ark

11. This person once danced before the ark

12. On the Day of Atonement, the High Priest sprinkled
    this on the ark

——— *Answer key on page 122.* ———

MONEY BIBLE VERSES

Pick the correct answer from the list provided.

A. ARROGANT   E. FIRSTFRUITS   I. RICH
B. DAILY   F. LITTLE   J. TAXES
C. DISHONEST   G. LOVE   K. TREASURE
D. ENOUGH   H. NAME   L. WEALTH

1. "Keep your lives free from the _____ of money and be content" (Hebrews 13:5).

2. "_____ money dwindles away" (Proverbs 13:11).

3. "Those who want to get _____ fall into temptation and a trap" (1 Timothy 6:9).

4. "The blessing of the LORD brings _____, without painful toil for it" (Proverbs 10:22).

5. "Whoever loves money never has _____" (Ecclesiastes 5:10).

6. "Honor the LORD with your wealth, with the _____ of all your crops" (Proverbs 3:9).

7. "Better a _____ with the fear of the LORD than great wealth with turmoil" (Proverbs 15:16).

8. "For where your _____ is, there your heart will be also" (Matthew 6:21).

9. "Command those who are rich in this present world not to be _____" (1 Timothy 6:17).

10. "Give me neither poverty nor riches, but give me only my _____ bread" (Proverbs 30:8).

11. "A good _____ is more desirable than great riches" (Proverbs 22:1).

12. "This is also why you pay _____, for the authorities are God's servants" (Romans 13:6).

—— Answer key on page 122. ——

PROPHECIES ABOUT JESUS CROSSWORD

"This has all taken place that the writings of the prophets might be fulfilled." —Matthew 26:56

Across

4. He would be _____ in Bethlehem.

6. He would come from the line of this patriarch.

8. He would _____ from the dead.

10. He would ride into Zion on this.

12. His hands and feet would be _____.

13. He would be from this tribe.

16. He would commit His _____ to the Father.

17. He would be sold for this many pieces of silver.

18. He would be called the rejected _____ stone.

19. He would go to this African country.

Down

1. Jesus would have no broken _____.

2. He would ask God why He had _____ Him.

3. Because of his hometown, He would be called this.

5. He would be given this man's throne.

7. His betrayer would buy a potter's _____.

9. He would receive the title "Man of _____."

11. He would be buried among these people.

14. His mother would be this.

15. He would sit at God's _____ hand.

17. On the cross He would become very _____.

"A" MEN

Provide the answer for the person being described.
All names start with the letter "A."

1. Moses's brother.

2. Another name for Azariah, friend of Daniel.

3. Son of David; died when his hair got stuck in a tree.

4. Paul attempted to persuade this king to become a Christian.

5. Peter's brother and fellow disciple.

6. Husband of Priscilla.

7. Psalm writer whose feet almost slipped.

8. First murder victim in history.

9. His name means "of the ground."

10. Biblical prophet who lived near Tekoa.

11. He and his wife died for lying to the church.

12. The eighth son of Jacob. Mother was Zilpah.

WHERE DOES THIS BOOK BELONG?

Choose the correct Bible section for each of these books. Some will be used more than once.

A. LAW
B. HISTORY
C. MAJOR PROPHETS

D. POETRY (WISDOM)
E. MINOR PROPHETS

____ 1. Exodus

____ 7. Job

____ 2. Amos

____ 8. Deuteronomy

____ 3. Proverbs

____ 9. Song of Songs

____ 4. 1 Kings

____ 10. Jeremiah

____ 5. Isaiah

____ 11. Leviticus

____ 6. Malachi

____ 12. Daniel

APOSTLE PAUL CROSSWORD

*"Paul, called to be an apostle of Christ Jesus
by the will of God." —1 Corinthians 1:1*

Across

  1. Paul argued with this disciple over circumcision.

  6. Paul's name before he was converted.

  7. The Jewish tribe Paul was born into.

  8. City from which Paul departed for missionary journeys.

  9. Town where Paul was born.

10. Judge who said to Paul, "you are out of your mind."

12. Paul was present at this man's stoning.

14. Paul's religion before he met Jesus.

15. Paul's religion teacher before meeting Jesus.

17. Where Paul wrote the Epistles while under arrest.

19. Paul spent three years here after conversion.

Down

  2. Paul's nationality.

  3. Where Paul was going when he met Jesus.

  4. Paul's companion on his first missionary journey.

  5. The affliction Paul suffered at his conversion.

  6. Paul's companion on his second missionary journey.

11. The profession by which Paul had earned a living.

13. Number of missionary journeys Paul took.

16. The people Paul arrested and threw in jail.

18. Island where Paul was shipwrecked.

GOD'S ATTRIBUTES
WORD SEARCH

Words may be horizontal, vertical, or diagonal, forward or backward, and may overlap.

```
M  Z  H  N  Q  S  T  P  F  U  N  Z  R  A  F
I  S  A  K  L  V  O  W  A  O  D  U  S  M  E
O  M  W  J  O  O  E  V  S  T  Y  O  H  X  T
W  M  M  J  O  M  V  L  E  U  I  X  O  Z  E
M  G  N  A  U  T  N  E  B  R  O  E  E  G  R
Q  A  R  I  N  S  N  I  Y  A  E  L  N  T  N
C  E  J  A  P  E  T  E  S  Q  T  I  A  T  A
J  T  M  E  C  R  N  E  T  C  B  U  G  E  L
S  R  R  A  S  I  E  T  T  O  I  G  M  N  J
H  U  M  J  E  T  O  S  W  I  P  E  L  M  B
O  T  P  Z  V  F  I  U  E  I  N  I  N  C  I
L  H  Z  A  Z  O  L  C  S  N  S  I  N  T  T
Y  Q  F  P  E  R  F  E  C  T  T  E  F  M  J
T  R  A  N  S  C  E  N  D  E  N  T  L  N  O
J  O  Q  Z  C  N  P  E  R  S  O  N  A  L  I
```

ETERNAL	JUST	PERSONAL
GOOD	LOVE	SOVEREIGN
GRACIOUS	MAJESTIC	TRANSCENDENT
HOLY	OMNIPOTENT	TRUTH
IMMANENT	OMNIPRESENT	WISE
IMMUTABLE	OMNISCIENT	
INFINITE	PATIENT	
JEALOUS	PERFECT	

—— Answer key on page 124. ——

WHAT THE HOLY SPIRIT DOES
WORD SEARCH

Words may be horizontal, vertical, or diagonal, forward or backward, and may overlap.

```
I  E  G  U  A  R  A  N  T  E  E  S  X  S  T
T  E  A  C  H  E  S  H  F  A  P  T  Y  K  E
G  A  R  X  D  N  P  R  E  L  S  A  S  W  S
O  Y  I  A  R  G  W  B  C  L  R  W  E  O  T
S  T  C  E  R  I  D  G  O  P  P  U  I  I  I
F  V  H  E  Q  U  W  G  N  A  H  S  F  N  F
B  A  P  T  I  Z  E  S  V  V  R  Z  I  I  I
C  Y  S  O  F  C  N  I  I  Q  E  E  T  L  E
U  O  G  R  I  Q  N  Z  C  N  G  B  C  L  S
F  H  M  E  E  D  Z  C  T  Q  E  C  N  U  E
C  G  B  F  W  W  R  T  S  Q  N  Q  A  M  D
G  C  W  E  O  E  O  L  N  D  E  T  S  I  E
J  C  L  B  A  R  A  P  F  O  R  Y  L  N  C
X  L  L  T  E  E  T  H  M  T  A  S  L  E  R
S  Y  E  N  S  Z  A  S  Y  E  T  A  I  S  E
G  S  E  R  I  P  S  N  I  F  E  X  F  T  T
A  W  G  T  J  V  J  U  I  B  S  C  C  H  N
S  R  E  X  Q  J  X  G  G  Q  O  U  P  N  I
```

BAPTIZES	GIFTS	PRAYS
COMFORTS	GUARANTEES	REGENERATES
CONVICTS	HELPS	RENEWS
CREATES	ILLUMINES	SANCTIFIES
DIRECTS	INDWELLS	SEALS
EMPOWERS	INSPIRES	TEACHES
FILLS	INTERCEDES	TESTIFIES

SPELL CHECK

Select the proper spelling for the following biblical names or terms.

___ 1. a. Amelakites
     b. Amellekites
     c. Amalekites

___ 7. a. malisious
     b. malishious
     c. malicious

___ 2. a. Messpatamia
     b. Mesopotamia
     c. Mesopatamia

___ 8. a. Abendago
     b. Abbenego
     c. Abednego

___ 3. a. Jehoshaphat
     b. Jehasafat
     c. Jehosephat

___ 9. a. Saducees
     b. Sadducees
     c. Sadduces

___ 4. a. syngogue
     b. synagogue
     c. synegogue

___ 10. a. Abimilek
     b. Abemelech
     c. Abimelek

___ 5. a. genneology
     b. genealogy
     c. genyalogy

___ 11. a. Philippians
     b. Phillipians
     c. Philippiuns

___ 6. a. Epaphroditus
     b. Epafrodties
     c. Ephaphratitus

___ 12. a. Eccleseastes
     b. Eclesiastes
     c. Ecclesiastes

—— *Answer key on page 124.* ——

WORDS FROM REVELATION SCRAMBLE

Unscramble the following words that come from the book of Revelation.

1. crypehpo _____

2. huhccr _____

3. nvees _____

4. aahjlelulh _____

5. yotwhr _____

6. malb _____

7. gsaenl _____

8. ioivns _____

9. voilnereta _____

10. wlkueamr _____

11. nliuattbior _____

12. otehrn _____

13. delesr _____

14. lorslc _____

15. assle _____

16. peutmrts _____

17. egdjtunm _____

18. sabet _____

19. naeehv _____

20. ehart _____

—— Answer key on page 125. ——

MATTHEW 1–14 CROSSWORD

"Then Jesus came to them and said, 'All authority in heaven and on earth has been given to me.'" —Matthew 28:18.

Across

1. Where John baptized people.

5. John said he was unworthy to carry these of Jesus.

7. First patriarch mentioned in Matthew's genealogy.

8. The physical problem of Peter's mother-in-law that Jesus healed.

10. They asked Jesus: "Why do you speak . . . in parables?"

12. What Herod told the Magi he wanted to do regarding Jesus.

14. In one word, the message of John the Baptist.

15. Jesus said, "It is not the healthy who need a doctor, but the ____."

16. Jesus said of this leader: "I have not found anyone . . . with such great faith."

17. Where Joseph and Mary were to escape with the baby.

18. Days Jesus fasted before facing Satan's temptation.

19. In the Gadarenes, Jesus sent demons into these.

Down

2. How the Magi discovered not to go back to Herod.

3. When Jesus walked on water, the disciples thought they saw one of these.

4. In the genealogy he was the son of Ruth and grandfather of David.

5. Joseph was to name the baby "Jesus," for He would ____ the people from their sins.

6. At Jesus's baptism, the Spirit descended like one of these.

9. Joseph is referred to as a ____ man.

11. The genealogy lists three sets of this many generations.

13. Jesus harvested this on the Sabbath which upset the Pharisees.

15. When Jesus heard of John the Baptist's death, He went to a ____ place.

18. Jesus said to the woman who was healed after touching His hem, "Your ____ has healed you."

HE MARRIED WHOM? CROSSWORD

Do you remember the wives of these men?

Across

5. Nabal

6. Boaz

7. Ananias

8. Isaac

10. Joseph (New Testament)

13. Ahasuerus

14. Amram

Down

1. Aquila

2. David

3. Elkanah

4. Elimelek

7. Zebedee

9. Zechariah

11. Hosea

12. Ahab

15. Adam

COMMANDS FROM GOD

Match the task mentioned with the person God told to carry out that command. Some will be used more than once.

A. ABRAHAM D. GIDEON G. MOSES
B. DAVID   E. JACOB   H. SAMUEL
C. ELIJAH   F. JOSHUA

___ 1. Take off your shoes.

___ 2. Offer your son as a burnt offering.

___ 3. Speak to the rock.

___ 4. Go to Hebron.

___ 5. Go across the Jordan.

___ 6. Tell the soldiers, "Whoever is afraid, go home."

___ 7. Look at the heart, not appearance.

___ 8. Hide by the Brook Kerith.

___ 9. Go to Bethel and live there.

___ 10. March around a city to defeat it.

Answer key on page 126.

JUST ONE BOOK

Each of these men and women appear in only one book of the Bible. Match the person with the book:

A. GENESIS
B. JOSHUA
C. JUDGES
D. RUTH
E. 1 SAMUEL
F. 2 SAMUEL

G. 1 KINGS
H. 1 CHRONICLES
I. NEHEMIAH
J. JOB
K. PROVERBS
L. DANIEL

M. LUKE
N. JOHN
O. ACTS
P. ROMANS
Q. 1 CORINTHIANS
R. 2 TIMOTHY

____ 1. Nicodemus

____ 2. Delilah

____ 3. Achan

____ 4. Sanballat

____ 5. Chloe

____ 6. Ben-Hur

____ 7. Agrippa

____ 8. Claudia

____ 9. Jabez

____ 10. Joanna

____ 11. Ichabod

____ 12. Lemuel

____ 13. Julia

____ 14. Esau

____ 15. Naomi

____ 16. Mephibosheth

____ 17. Abednego

____ 18. Bildad

Answer key on page 126.

OLD TESTAMENT TOWNS AND CITIES
WORD SEARCH

*Words may be horizontal, vertical, or diagonal,
forward or backward, and may overlap.*

```
G L J B G B E E R S H E B A Q
P E E Y I W E J O T C Q S W V
R W K L B C D T W Y W Q L G S
K A M R E J B Q H R W D A A A
N A W F O C O F Y E K I C Z M
P B T N N R P S S L E H A A
Q W I Q V I A L P F D D I Y R
S H I L O H E S G A A H S A I
M S H E C H E M H A N B H S A
J E R U S A L E M K T Y H H S
Q W M E G I D D O X E H C D I
G I B E A H E V I V E L S O D
I Z A M I I W F L A C D O D O
W T X Q N J E R I C H O L N N
R E H E B R O N U A R A D P H
```

ARAD	EKRON	JERICHO	SHECHEM
ASHDOD	GATH	JERUSALEM	SHILOH
ASHKELON	GAZA	JOPPA	SIDON
BEERSHEBA	GIBEAH	LACHISH	TYRE
BETHEL	GIBEON	MEGIDDO	
DAN	HEBRON	SAMARIA	

LEVITICUS
WORD SEARCH

Words may be horizontal, vertical, or diagonal, forward or backward, and may overlap.

```
T A O G E P A C S O R P N U F
S L A V I T S E F F L O H T E
L J T S N S C H E F J S Z H C
K M N Z I E F J S E P S T A I
X L Q L A W W S D R U Y D N F
G P G T R C E K Y I H H C K I
T U R L G N A O N A E H S R
R N I I I O N G G N R X G C
O X E L E L G L I S D I V I A
B G O M T S E R E S F U D V S
H H Z B E V T P Z Q N R Y I D
G O A T I N J S G Z L A W N W
I W W T H U O T I T H E E G R
E N E A B W H T A B B A S L B
N S H I N O R A A R O M A U C
L P L P A S S O V E R S R X P
E E L E P R O S Y E Q N W X D
E W O R S H I P G A T T B E A
```

AARON	GRAIN	LEVITES	SCAPEGOAT
AROMA	GUILT	NEIGHBOR	THANKSGIVING
ATONEMENT	HOLINESS	OFFERINGS	TITHE
BURNT	HYSSOP	PASSOVER	WORSHIP
CLEANSING	INCENSE	PRIESTS	
EPHAH	JUBILEE	SABBATH	
FESTIVALS	LEPROSY	SACRIFICE	

Note: These terms are from various Bible translations.

——— *Answer key on page 127.* ———

MICHAEL OR GABRIEL?

The archangels Michael and Gabriel were active in the Bible story. Which one was involved or will be in these situations?

A. MICHAEL   B. GABRIEL   C. BOTH

____ 1. Argued with the devil over Moses's body.

____ 2. Announced to the shepherds that Jesus was born.

____ 3. Told Zechariah (Luke 1) that he would be a father.

____ 4. Will represent Israel in the tribulation.

____ 5. In Revelation 12:7, he fought against the dragon.

____ 6. Helped get a prayer to Daniel.

____ 7. Explained to Daniel about the 70-weeks prophecy.

____ 8. Explained to Daniel the Ram and Goat vision.

——— *Answer key on page 127.* ———

BOOKS OF THE BIBLE SCRAMBLE

Unscramble the following words that come from the books of the Bible.

1. bkakhuka _____

2. leihompn _____

3. wmeahtt _____

4. elcrcinsoh _____

5. soxdeu _____

6. iharemje _____

7. voailneret _____

8. telosnsasainh _____

9. ghgaia _____

10. tseiotannmal _____

11. hoitytm _____

12. oracntishin _____

13. yretumoedno _____

14. iehnheam _____

15. siphpliapin _____

16. hibodaa _____

17. camhlia _____

18. sehapensi _____

19. velicstui _____

20. wreeshb _____

——— Answer key on page 128. ———

GOD IS . . .
WORD SEARCH

Words may be horizontal, vertical, or diagonal, forward or backward, and may overlap.

```
J  U  S  T  A  U  U  T  O  G  D  I  Z  X  A
R  I  G  H  T  E  O  U  S  R  S  D  L  X  Z
Y  B  G  H  B  W  I  S  E  A  O  S  O  I  N
U  D  O  T  R  U  E  J  B  C  V  P  V  N  O
L  Z  O  C  T  Y  J  M  K  I  E  I  E  F  M
G  I  D  P  P  N  L  E  V  O  R  R  U  I  N
L  M  G  C  L  E  E  O  P  U  E  I  D  N  I
O  M  X  H  L  L  R  S  H  S  I  T  W  I  P
R  U  J  P  T  U  U  F  E  R  G  U  F  T  O
I  T  D  K  B  Z  F  F  E  R  N  T  K  E  T
O  A  G  S  D  P  Z  I  H  C  P  B  L  N  E
U  B  G  K  I  B  D  O  C  T  T  I  E  J  N
S  L  E  T  E  R  N  A  L  R  I  L  N  N  T
G  E  C  R  Q  S  W  L  Q  H  E  A  J  M  O
V  O  M  N  I  S  C  I  E  N  T  M  F  Z  O
```

ETERNAL	IMMUTABLE	OMNIPOTENT	SOVEREIGN
FAITHFUL	INFINITE	OMNIPRESENT	SPIRIT
GLORIOUS	JUST	OMNISCIENT	TRUE
GOOD	LIGHT	ONE	WISE
GRACIOUS	LOVE	PERFECT	
HOLY	MERCIFUL	RIGHTEOUS	

Answer key on page 128.

WORD SEARCH

Words may be horizontal, vertical, or diagonal,
forward or backward, and may overlap.

```
J  F  N  M  A  N  G  E  R  M  S  A  N  D  T
F  M  E  F  C  L  I  F  F  K  M  P  I  S  R
U  P  G  A  A  M  H  D  O  E  A  N  M  I  U
R  S  M  D  T  W  V  A  O  R  N  M  N  A  M
R  P  N  M  E  H  N  H  R  W  E  K  B  H  P
O  S  O  O  A  E  E  O  D  N  I  C  H  A  E
W  N  S  N  G  V  K  R  X  J  E  N  E  W  T
Z  O  T  T  L  O  F  S  S  Y  M  S  G  K  M
V  R  R  H  E  X  N  E  R  U  Y  U  S  S  H
S  T  I  S  Y  U  P  A  S  T  U  R  E  C  S
Y  I  C  T  Q  U  I  V  E  R  D  S  V  R  T
Q  N  H  S  A  L  T  F  L  A  T  S  Y  A  O
E  G  G  S  F  L  I  G  H  T  S  I  S  G  R
K  P  H  W  X  P  G  O  A  T  S  T  O  D  K
L  O  C  U  S  T  R  F  D  O  N  K  E  Y  D
```

CLIFF	FEATHERS	LOCUST	QUIVER
CRAG	FLIGHT	MANE	SALTFLATS
DOE	FURROW	MANGER	SAND
DONKEY	GOATS	MONTHS	SNORTING
EAGLE	HARNESS	OSTRICH	STORK
EGGS	HAWK	OX	TRUMPET
FAWN	HORSE	PASTURE	WINGS

PSALMS CROSSWORD

"I praise you because I am fearfully and wonderfully made; your works are wonderful, I know that full well." —Psalm 139:14

Across

3. In the darkest valley, we don't fear this (23:4).

5. 176 of these in Psalm 119.

7. The fear of the Lord is the beginning of this (111:10).

11. The Psalms have 150 of these.

13. Animal that pants for water (42:1).

15. The Lord is our light and this (27:1).

17. Out of a pit and onto this (Psalm 40:2).

18. Blessed is the person whose delight is in this (Psalm 1:1–2).

19. Songs sung while going up to Jerusalem.

21. A psalm that is a cry of anguish.

22. In anger, don't do this (Psalm 4:4).

23. The Lord in heaven does this at leaders who reject him (2:4).

24. The literary form of the Psalms.

Down

1. They are "a little lower than the angels" (8:4–5).

2. This declares the glory of God (19:1).

4. Just like the Pentateuch, Psalm can be divided into this many sections.

6. Offspring are this (Psalm 127:3).

8. Psalm 8:1: "How _____ is [God's] name."

9. He wrote the most psalms.

10. God's Word, which stands firm in heaven, is this (119:89).

11. Where Jesus was when he quoted Psalm 22:1.

12. Many psalms end with this word of unknown meaning.

14. Most-mentioned musical instrument.

16. What we lack with the Lord as shepherd (23:1).

20. The meaning of the word "psalm."

21. God's Word is this for our feet (119:105).

23. The most frequent word in the Psalms.

WHAT TO WEAR

Who wore or will wear the following garments mentioned in the Bible? (Some are groups, not individuals.)

1. A scarlet robe given him by soldiers

2. An ephod

3. A white robe

4. A multi-colored coat

5. Camel-hair clothes

6. Leaves

7. A robe with a corner cut out

8. A little robe made by his mother

9. A cloak he left at Troas

10. A linen robe that matched the robes of the men carrying the ark of the covenant

—— Answer key on page 129. ——

NOAH AND THE ARK
WORD SEARCH

*Words may be horizontal, vertical, or diagonal,
forward or backward, and may overlap.*

```
N A A C R E A T U R E S W E B Z
L A M E C H X T C N A N J E D J
Z F L O O D W A T E R S A O E P
Y R I G H T E O U S C R P H C I
V I O L E N C E M K H A H Y K T
B L A M E L E S S C D V E T S C
C O V E N A N T W Y O E T R F H
D J E Y F A V O R P O N H O O Q
W I A V G K P I O R R A W O R W
M O U N T A I N S E J R R F T G
G H Q R A L N X B S I A Q F Y S
D C G R I E V E D S B R V X V H
O H I O C Q L H N Z F A A T I E
V O L S E V E N U S E T R T S M
E Y U W I C K E D N E S S P L Y
R A I N B O W C X H A M R B V A
```

ALTAR	DOOR	JAPHETH	ROOF
ARARAT	DOVE	LAMECH	SEVEN
BLAMELESS	FAVOR	MOUNTAINS	SHEM
COVENANT	FLOODWATERS	PITCH	VIOLENCE
CREATURES	FORTY	RAINBOW	WICKEDNESS
CYPRESS	GRIEVED	RAVEN	
DECKS	HAM	RIGHTEOUS	

GENESIS CROSSWORD

"God saw all that he had made, and it was very good."
—Genesis 1:31

Across

1. Husband and wife: One
   _____.

5. Day 6: Livestock, ground creatures, and these animals.

6. Condition God said man should not be in.

8. This was over the "surface of the deep."

9. Trees had fruit with these inside.

11. Creatures that guarded the garden.

13. What God called the time when light was over the earth.

16. Name of God's first garden.

18. The first water source for plants (Genesis 2).

22. What Adam did when he heard, "the sound of the Lord."

23. This appeared on the third day.

24. Craftiest wild animal in the garden.

Down

1. First description of earth.

2. Day 2: Water was separated from this.

3. The serpent was sentenced to do this.

4. God's description of created light.

7. After eating the fruit, Adam and Eve realized they were this.

10. What the serpent told Eve she wouldn't do.

12. Man was made in God's
    _____.

14. What God did on Day 7.

15. Creation day of water creatures and birds.

17. Plants bore seed according to their
    _____.

19. Part of Adam God used to make Eve.

20. Day 4: Greater light, lesser light—and these.

21. One of the first things created in Genesis 1:1.

BATTLE GEAR
WORD SEARCH

*Words may be horizontal, vertical, or diagonal,
forward or backward, and may overlap.*

```
L  J  W  W  C  H  H  S  X  A  G  O  L  A  J
E  I  S  I  C  K  L  E  H  S  W  O  R  D  M
W  F  F  Q  E  C  W  V  L  I  G  T  S  M  A
P  E  Q  S  F  F  H  K  Y  M  E  D  Q  N  T
E  R  A  X  X  R  A  A  T  L  E  L  Y  S  T
J  P  T  P  R  X  J  S  R  J  F  T  D  P  O
U  X  F  W  O  J  R  F  H  I  Z  U  Y  E  C
Z  P  G  U  I  N  I  Z  H  E  O  F  A  A  K
F  X  B  R  E  A  S  T  P  L  A  T  E  R  B
O  H  P  L  D  A  R  M  O  R  J  T  V  F  O
Q  A  R  R  O  W  C  U  V  X  R  U  H  G  W
J  Z  M  M  I  A  E  E  H  O  R  S  E  N  H
D  J  A  V  E  L  I  N  M  F  D  Y  A  U  E
M  L  A  X  E  S  K  W  H  G  V  I  Y  L  T
I  N  C  H  A  I  N  M  A  I  L  J  X  G  O
```

ARMOR	CHARIOT	MATTOCK	SWORD
ARROW	CHAINMAIL	SICKLE	WEAPON
AXES	HELMET	SHEATH	
BOW	HORSE	SHIELD	
BREASTPLATE	JAVELIN	SPEAR	

—— *Answer key on page 131.* ——

ALTAR BUILDERS
WORD SEARCH

Words may be horizontal, vertical, or diagonal, forward or backward, and may overlap.

```
A X J T Y Y S W W N T W D I A
C H F O N E L I J A H P W B B
I Q A O S I R U T M Q Z Y J R
B S D B B H M H N G O E I I A
J L A W T A U O Z I R R G V H
N A C A H Z L A S K F U R J A
U U C P C F M A B E M B S E M
G H R O M Q Z D K B S B V R A
I B Q I B I Q G Y M M A K O W
D M A N A S S E H A W B I B S
E V W Z M H J B P N V E O O A
O D M M W G J L L O I L G A T
N N M Z S A U L A A R O G M I
I I X N O A H A S H H C W X I
N S A M U E L L D A V I D B C
```

ABRAHAM	GIDEON	MANASSEH	SAUL
AHAB	ISAAC	MANOAH	URIAH
BALAK	JACOB	MOSES	ZERUBBABEL
DAVID	JEROBOAM	NOAH	
ELIJAH	JOSHUA	SAMUEL	

EVENTS IN JERUSALEM

*Provide the answers to these events that
occurred in Jerusalem.*

1. This king captured Jerusalem and made it the capital.

2. This son of David temporarily took over Jerusalem during King David's reign.

3. This person built the first temple in Jerusalem.

4. This king destroyed Jerusalem in 586 BC.

5. This ruler made a decree allowing the Jews to return to Jerusalem and rebuild it.

6. This man orchestrated rebuilding the walls of the city.

7. This Judean king rebuilt the temple in 20 BC.

8. This disciple preached his first sermon in Jerusalem at Pentecost.

9. This follower of Jesus became the first Christian martyr while in Jerusalem.

10. This person cleansed the temple in Jerusalem.

11. Jesus was arrested in this part of the city.

12. This structure was destroyed in AD 70.

EARLY CHURCHES
WORD SEARCH

*Words may be horizontal, vertical, or diagonal,
forward or backward, and may overlap.*

```
J  L  I  C  O  N  I  U  M  L  Y  C  M  M  E
J  E  P  H  E  Y  U  G  E  Y  G  C  R  D  C
P  S  R  E  F  L  M  A  R  S  N  O  Y  E  O
C  H  M  U  R  M  A  Y  Z  T  J  R  G  R  L
M  A  I  Y  S  G  T  O  A  R  K  I  A  B  O
R  H  N  L  R  A  A  C  D  A  C  N  L  E  S
V  U  F  T  A  N  L  M  R  I  C  T  A  Y  S
U  T  Z  L  I  D  A  E  U  L  C  H  T  K  A
R  O  M  E  Z  O  E  Q  M  M  E  E  I  C  E
T  R  O  A  S  N  C  L  O  I  I  A  A  P  I
R  S  A  R  D  I  S  H  P  Y  W  E  J  Q  I
J  T  H  Y  A  T  I  R  A  H  T  D  N  Z  X
R  C  K  K  Z  W  P  H  I  L  I  P  P  I  T
T  H  E  S  S  A  L  O  N  I  C  A  C  F  B
Y  P  T  R  Z  E  P  H  E  S  U  S  J  C  F
```

ANTIOCH	JERUSALEM	SARDIS
COLOSSAE	LAODICEA	SMYRNA
CORINTH	LYSTRA	THESSALONICA
DERBE	PERGAMUM	THYATIRA
EPHESUS	PHILADELPHIA	TROAS
GALATIA	PHILIPPI	
ICONIUM	ROME	

——— *Answer key on page 132.* ———

CALLED! CROSSWORD

"And we know that in all things God works for the good of those who love him, who have been called according to his purpose." —Romans 8:28

Across

4. Called to replace Eli.

6. Called to set his people free.

7. Called to rescue mankind from total annihilation.

8. Called to be a great king—a man after God's heart.

10. Called to be the first high priest of Israel.

11. Called to prepare the way for Jesus.

13. Called to be the first king of Israel.

14. Called to witness to a searching Ethiopian.

Down

1. Called to defeat the Midianites with a small army.

2. Called to take his people into their land.

3. Called to build a wall.

4. Called to be a deacon and a martyr.

5. Called to replace Judas.

9. Called to interpret a king's dreams.

12. Called to save her people from genocide.

SPIRITUAL GIFTS
WORD SEARCH

*Words may be horizontal, vertical, or diagonal,
forward or backward, and may overlap.*

```
V  R  I  S  K  N  O  W  L  E  D  G  E  K  H
E  P  C  Y  Q  J  T  C  L  T  I  Q  K  A  S
J  X  G  H  G  R  F  O  M  O  S  F  P  P  B
Q  O  H  H  E  X  Y  L  E  N  C  Q  M  O  N
G  Y  L  O  V  A  V  T  R  G  E  E  I  S  E
S  I  N  N  R  T  L  Z  C  U  R  X  N  T  V
P  T  V  W  G  T  Q  I  Y  E  N  B  I  L  A
A  F  A  I  T  H  A  E  N  S  M  T  S  E  N
S  T  Y  S  N  Q  H  T  X  G  E  E  T  S  G
T  J  N  U  T  G  O  T  I  R  N  A  E  H  E
O  K  C  J  P  L  S  F  N  O  T  C  R  I  L
R  Z  Y  I  B  H  R  L  F  A  N  H  I  P  I
V  B  D  P  R  O  P  H  E  C  Y  E  N  T  S
K  H  E  V  X  A  J  K  D  A  C  R  G  S  M
I  W  I  S  D  O  M  I  R  A  C  L  E  S  S
```

APOSTLESHIP	HEALING	PROPHECY
DISCERNMENT	KNOWLEDGE	TEACHER
EVANGELISM	MERCY	TONGUES
EXHORTATION	MINISTERING	WISDOM
FAITH	MIRACLES	
GIVING	PASTOR	

Answer key on page 133.

WHAT GOD GIVES THE BELIEVER
WORD SEARCH

*Words may be horizontal, vertical, or diagonal,
forward or backward, and may overlap.*

```
B G H I N S T R U C T I O N F
S Z Y M E R C Y C A R E U D P
T E M R S Q L M W V E K W F U
R A M D E Z V H S I F P I H R
E O S P S D D U K P U C S J I
N N D S O S E E R H G I D O F
G Y O G U W E M C E E T O R I
T F J I U R E N P A S L M E C
H R F U T I A R E T E T W W A
L E B S R C D N M V I P I A T
I E Z J O D E A C E I O K R I
F D J B Z H Q T N E N G N D O
E O A P O W E R O C V T R S N
E M B N T E C J X R E O F O E
R V F U T U R E A H P F L H F
```

ASSURANCE	INSTRUCTION	PURIFICATION
CARE	LIFE	REDEMPTION
EMPOWERMENT	LOVE	REFUGE
FORGIVENESS	MERCY	REST
FREEDOM	PEACE	REWARDS
FUTURE	POWER	STRENGTH
GUIDANCE	PROTECTION	WISDOM

LAST WORDS

Identify the person who said these last recorded biblical words.

1. "You are a man of wisdom; you will know what to do to [Shimei]. Bring his gray head down to the grave in blood."

2. "God will surely come to your aid, and then you must carry my bones up from this place."

3. "Please, God, strengthen me just once more, and let me with one blow get revenge on the Philistines for my two eyes."

4. "Draw your sword and run me through."

5. "This stone will be a witness against us. It has heard all the words the LORD has said to us. It will be a witness against you if you are untrue to your God."

6. "My lord, what will the outcome of all this ['a time, times and half a time'] be?"

7. "You will receive power when the Holy Spirit comes on you."*

8. "Lord, do not hold this sin against them."

9. "Grow in grace and knowledge of our Lord and Savior Jesus Christ. To him be glory both now and forever! Amen."

10. "Blessed are you, Israel! . . . Your enemies will cower before you, and you will tread on their hights."

He is quoted later, but not in a conversation scenario.

NAMES OF JESUS
WORD SEARCH

*Words may be horizontal, vertical, or diagonal,
forward or backward, and may overlap.*

```
M  E  S  S  I  A  H  K  I  A  C  B  C  D  M
R  V  I  D  S  C  B  N  A  D  G  E  D  F  J
B  E  F  T  O  Y  O  M  K  V  O  L  Y  P  U
F  R  S  O  D  Z  Z  M  Q  O  V  O  H  R  D
S  T  A  U  U  A  Y  W  M  C  E  V  M  I  G
H  F  T  N  R  N  Y  Y  S  A  R  E  I  N  E
E  U  T  E  C  R  D  S  D  T  N  D  G  C  J
P  K  W  B  D  H  E  A  P  E  O  D  I  E  G
H  S  J  N  C  O  D  C  T  R  R  A  E  S  U
E  C  N  P  C  H  O  R  T  I  I  M  F  R  I
R  Y  K  D  S  Y  R  R  O  I  O  N  L  C  D
D  L  A  M  B  R  X  I  C  C  O  N  G  Y  E
I  M  M  A  N  U  E  L  S  V  K  N  U  W  O
D  S  U  E  G  L  C  A  P  T  A  I  N  U  B
V  M  A  S  A  V  I  O  R  A  L  P  H  A  T
```

ADVOCATE	COMMANDER	JUDGE	SAVIOR
ALPHA	DAYSPRING	LAMB	SHEPHERD
BELOVED	DOOR	MESSIAH	
BRANCH	FOUNDATION	PRINCE	
CAPTAIN	GOVERNOR	RESURRECTION	
CHRIST	IMMANUEL	ROCK	

Note: These terms are from various Bible translations.

—— *Answer key on page 134.* ——

MORE NAMES OF JESUS
WORD SEARCH

Words may be horizontal, vertical, or diagonal, forward or backward, and may overlap.

```
T  A  U  A  P  L  K  P  Y  M  N  M  E  V  P
E  N  R  M  B  R  Y  A  T  E  B  A  F  I  Q
A  S  N  E  P  G  I  V  K  D  P  S  S  N  J
C  B  A  N  D  M  L  E  T  I  R  T  M  E  S
H  O  I  C  A  E  F  L  S  A  O  E  C  G  T
E  F  U  S  R  A  E  M  O  T  P  R  N  O  O
R  D  I  N  H  I  N  M  J  O  I  U  G  I  N
J  Q  Q  L  S  O  F  O  E  R  T  W  D  U  E
G  A  M  O  I  E  P  I  I  R  I  P  A  S  O
X  F  J  R  P  G  L  C  C  N  A  X  O  Y  L
L  A  M  B  D  V  H  O  U  E  T  D  E  B  I
J  E  H  O  V  A  H  T  R  O  I  E  U  T  T
V  C  A  R  P  E  N  T  E  R  O  E  D  K  C
D  R  I  T  W  O  R  D  Q  V  N  J  O  W  Q
N  A  Z  A  R  E  N  E  R  A  B  B  I  X  R
```

AMEN	LAMB	PROPITIATION	VINE
ANOINTED	LIGHT	RABBI	WORD
BISHOP	MASTER	REDEEMER	WAY
CARPENTER	MEDIATOR	SACRIFICE	
COUNSELOR	NAZARENE	STONE	
JEHOVAH	PRIEST	TEACHER	

Note: These terms are from various Bible translations.

BIBLE MISSIONARIES, PASTORS, AND EVANGELISTS

Name the person referred to in these descriptions.

1. This man accompanied Paul on his second missionary journey.

2. He was known as the forerunner of Jesus.

3. This man was called "righteous" by God, who then told him to warn the people about impending judgment.

4. Some call this man the world's greatest missionary ever. Before that he persecuted Christians.

5. When God called this man to witness for Him, he went the other way—before God got his attention.

6. This historian accompanied Paul on one of his missionary journeys—and wrote about it in the Bible.

7. This man went with Paul on his first missionary journey.

8. Directed by a vision, this man led a man from Africa to faith in Jesus.

9. When this man taught, some people said they were following him and some said they were following Paul.

10. On Paul's first missionary journey, this man deserted the mission before it was over.

—— *Answer key on page 134.* ——

PSALM VERSE FILL-IN CROSSWORD

*"Give thanks to the LORD, for he is good.
His love endures forever." —Psalm 136:1*

Across

3. "Your word is a _____ for my feet" (Psalm 119:105).

5. "The LORD watches over the way of the _____" (Psalm 1:6).

8. "The stone the builders rejected has become the _____" (Psalm 118:22).

10. "How good and pleasant it is when God's people live together in _____" (Psalm 133:1).

11. "Create in me a _____ heart, O God" (Psalm 51:10).

13. "Take delight in the LORD and he will give you the _____ of your heart" (Psalm 37:4).

15. "_____ say in their hearts, 'There is no God'" (Psalm 14:1 NLT).

Down

1. "_____ are a heritage from the LORD" (Psalm 127:3).

2. "I lift up my eyes to the mountains—where does my _____ come from?" (Psalm 121:1)

4. "Oh, how I love your law! I _____ on it all day long" (Psalm 119:97).

6. "Taste and see that the LORD is _____" (Psalm 34:8).

7. "Your word, LORD, is _____; it stands firm in the heavens" (Psalm 119:89).

9. "Teach us to _____ our days, that we may gain a heart of wisdom" (Psalm 90:12).

11. "Where can I go from your Spirit? Where can I flee from your _____" (Psalm 139:7).

12. "I praise you because I am _____ and wonderfully made" (Psalm 139:14).

14. "Whoever dwells in the shelter of the Most High will rest in the _____ of the Almighty" (Psalm 91:1).

Words may be horizontal, vertical, or diagonal, forward or backward, and may overlap.

```
P R E S E R V E H T O V S I J
R S L S Y U E F R E E D O M U
U T T N R K L G Q H R L U X D
W Y R A I I G Y D L O U O S G
C O S O T N G R E E N P U R M
O P N A F U O H A C L R E B E
M R O D L M T I T C I W A N N
M O B D E V O E S E I O O E T
A M E L E R A C S S O O J N L
N I Y O N L F T E E A U U E K
D S Q V B L I U I R E P S S R
S E H E Q H H G L O U R M G B
H C F T E A C H H W N P C O U
T H A N K S X Y L T N T G E C
S D L E L U G O N K N N T E D
```

COMFORT	GRACIOUS	OBEY	SALVATION
COMMANDS	HOPE	PRESERVE	STATUTES
COMPASSION	JUDGMENT	PROMISE	TEACH
DELIGHT	KNOWLEDGE	PURE	THANKS
DECREES	LEARN	REJOICE	WONDERFUL
FREEDOM	LOVE	RIGHTEOUS	

WEIGHTS AND MEASURES
WORD SEARCH

Words may be horizontal, vertical, or diagonal, forward or backward, and may overlap.

```
K N G P L H Y L L S G X H Y K
M O O V A D J Z E S P A E S F
C U B I T C A H Q R D A Q H S
C W I C A B E X H Z O H N E F
D O D F E K P R E E D A D K A
M D R E U A N J N K Q N B E T
U Y H I N R A U L D Y D E L H
F Z P C F E L W Z N Z B K N O
H U Q M I C H O N I Z R A W M
M I L E Q A E O N P K E H C B
T M A B W F P P M G Z A U Z L
Z H N M A N E H H E Y D O G G
D T A L W Q K N P A R T R A C
R B A T H V X G X B H H S I I
M E A S U R E W B O M E R K R
```

BATH	FURLONG	MILE
CAB	HANDBREADTH	OMER
COR	HIN	PACE
CUBIT	HOMER	REED
EPHAH	MANEH	SHEKEL
FATHOM	MEASURE	SPAN

BIBLE MOUNTAINS
WORD SEARCH

*Words may be horizontal, vertical, or diagonal,
forward or backward, and may overlap.*

```
C C A R M E L C Q J A W A L A
G B Q S H G S Z O N T V B E R
E G X E J Z I H A R A B A B A
R Z U I A T P L E L C B R A R
I K Y R X A I H E P M D I N A
Z O E W G B S A P A H O M O T
I Z L P I O G L E T D E N N K
M F F I H R A A B B H R O X
J F C H V R H K W E A S G Z B
Y O H O R E O I F I R L G I J
C M O M R Z S N I I A M E O L
V Y S L Y Q X N E B O R O N I
I A B S I N A I M I Z A R N D
T H H M O R I A H M K X B B T
Y X G I L B O A H O R E B I P
```

ABARIM	GILBOA	LEBANON	SEIR
ARARAT	GILEAD	MIZAR	SHEPHER
CARMEL	HALAK	MORIAH	SINAI
EBAL	HERMON	NEBO	TABOR
EPHRON	HOR	OLIVES	ZALMON
GERIZIM	HOREB	PISGAH	ZION

BIBLE-TIME PROFESSIONS
WORD SCRAMBLE

Unscramble the following Bible-time professions.

1. sonam   _____

2. nitrape   _____

3. rsesamsest   _____

4. mckrarbkie   _____

5. atennr   _____

6. engredar   _____

7. scunmaii   _____

8. pimperhotsc   _____

9. virtemslihs   _____

10. torail   _____

11. trubel   _____

12. ravewe   _____

13. ottrpe   _____

14. weerjel   _____

15. innpser   _____

MIRACLES HAPPEN CROSSWORD

"You are the God who performs miracles." —Psalm 77:14

Across

2. New mother at 90.
3. They fed Elijah at Kerith Ravine.
6. They rolled a heavy and heavily guarded stone away from the tomb.
8. Idol that fell in the presence of the ark of the covenant.
9. Angels opened doors to this for the disciples.
11. This fell after Joshua followed God's instructions to walk around it.
15. Balaam's donkey did this.
16. Elisha pours out unlimited oil for her.
17. Where Elijah called down fire onto watery altars.
18. Tongues of this hovered above disciples at Pentecost.
20. This fell over Jerusalem in mid-afternoon at Jesus's death.
21. At Belshazzar's party, writing appeared on this.

Down

1. The person Peter raised from the dead.
2. Moses's rod became this.
4. This opened up so Joshua and the people could enter the Promised Land.
5. He interpreted Pharaoh's dreams.
7. This suddenly appeared above Jonah for shade.
10. Twice Moses got water from these.
12. Elijah's vehicle to heaven.
13. Israelites were healed by looking at this on a pole
14. Temple item that tore in two at Jesus's death.
16. God provided this for Hagar in the desert.
18. It became wet when Gideon put it on the threshing floor overnight.
19. Where the world's languages began.

POSITIVE COMMANDS IN SCRIPTURE

Fill in the blanks.

1. "Be prepared to give an _____ to everyone who asks you to give the reason for the hope that you have" (1 Peter 3:15).

2. "Help the weak, be _____ with everyone" (1 Thessalonians 5:14).

3. "Live in _____ with one another" (Romans 12:16).

4. "Be filled with the _____" (Ephesians 5:18).

5. "Be _____ with what you have" (Hebrews 13:5).

6. "Cast all your _____ on [God]" (1 Peter 5:7).

7. "Always [give] _____ to God the Father for everything" (Ephesians 5:20).

8. "Let your _____ shine before others" (Matthew 5:16).

9. "Let your conversation be always full of _____" (Colossians 4:6).

10. "Approach God's throne of grace with _____" (Hebrews 4:16).

11. "Put on the full _____ of God" (Ephesians 6:13).

12. "[Make] the most of every _____" (Ephesians 5:16).

13. "Offer your bodies as a living _____" (Romans 12:1).

14. "Put on the new _____" (Ephesians 4:24).

BOOK OF ESTHER
WORD SEARCH

*Words may be horizontal, vertical, or diagonal,
forward or backward, and may overlap.*

```
S  I  G  N  E  T  T  G  A  R  D  E  N  K  M
C  Y  X  E  R  X  E  S  Z  H  L  P  H  L  U
D  I  G  H  M  E  M  U  K  A  N  E  A  P  K
M  N  T  W  M  H  Z  A  E  M  K  R  D  P  P
X  Y  L  A  L  O  C  W  X  A  L  S  A  E  E
B  B  R  T  D  I  R  W  I  N  C  I  S  R  H
P  A  L  R  E  E  T  D  L  G  E  A  S  F  E
W  E  N  D  H  N  L  Y  E  R  T  R  A  U  G
L  N  R  Q  D  I  I  R  S  C  E  B  H  M  A
Y  H  K  I  U  E  T  W  E  W  A  H  X  E  I
C  H  M  A  S  E  C  H  A  T  O  I  T  S  K
V  A  D  I  I  H  T  R  S  I  P  L  Q  S  G
C  U  S  H  R  D  H  Z  E  A  D  E  L  P  E
W  L  U  U  O  U  N  W  K  E  V  E  C  A  G
H  V  M  X  S  T  P  I  L  Z  V  O  M  S  G
```

BANQUET	HADASSAH	MYRRH	SUSA
CITADEL	HAMAN	PERFUMES	VASHTI
CUSH	HEGAI	PERISH	WINE
DECREE	INDIA	PERSIA	XERXES
ESTHER	MEDIA	PURIM	
EXILE	MEMUKAN	SCEPTER	
GARDEN	MORDECAI	SIGNET	

PLANTS OF THE BIBLE
WORD SEARCH

Words may be horizontal, vertical, or diagonal, forward or backward, and may overlap.

```
Q A G R C H R O S E W L L E M
C C U G O U R D P J W C S A Y
U B M O H J Q R U S H A B Y R
M B V A Z Z O H O S G L V V R
I F C T N I N U C J M A V V H
N O N A W D B H A Z K M F I G
Z J Q R V F R U A I M U J N T
F K X E A L C A L D F S T E H
P D K S C M W D K R Q L W N I
W O R M W O O D C E U P A T S
D G B K S C A R L E T S T X T
U I A N K Z I T Z M E Q H P L
C Z L L J Y L P H E N N A X E
P X M L L T L E E K S W J U Q
B R I E R S G R A S S E Z P X
```

BALM	FLAX	MANDRAKE	THISTLE
BRIERS	GALL	MYRRH	VINE
BULRUSH	GOURD	ROSE	WORMWOOD
CALAMUS	GRASS	RUSH	
CUMIN	HENNA	SCARLET	
DILL	LEEKS	TARES	

BIBLE VERSE FILL-IN

Fill in the blanks.

1. "The fear of the LORD is the beginning of
   _____" (Proverbs 1:7).

2. "You are to be _____ to me because I, the
   LORD, am _____" (Leviticus 20:26).

3. "Have I not commanded you? Be _____ and
   courageous" (Joshua 1:9).

4. "When the angel of the LORD appeared to Gideon, he
   said, 'The LORD is with you, mighty _____'"
   (Judges 6:12).

5. "To obey is better than _____, and to heed is
   better than the fat of rams" (1 Samuel 15:22).

6. "If my people, who are called by my name, will
   _____ themselves and pray and seek my face
   and turn from their wicked ways, then I will hear from
   heaven" (2 Chronicles 7:14).

7. "The heavens declare the _____ of God; the skies
   proclaim the _____ of his hands" (Psalm 19:1).

8. "Worship the LORD's with _____; come before
   him with joyful songs" (Psalm 100:2).

9. "Because of the LORD's great love we are not consumed,
   for his _____ never fail" (Lamentations
   3:22–23).

10. "A wife of noble character who can find? She is worth
    more than _____" (Proverbs 31:10).

11. "The _____ is plentiful, but the
    _____ are few" (Luke 10:2).

12. "Everyone who calls on the name of the Lord will be
    _____" (Romans 10:13).

—— Answer key on page 138. ——

ACTS 10-17 CROSSWORD

"The word of the Lord spread through the whole region."
—Acts 13:49

Across

4. King who put Peter in prison.

6. Some expressed surprise that these people could be saved.

8. What the Jews in Thessalonica started in protest to Paul's message.

10. Peter saw a sheet with these on it.

11. Seller of purple in Philippi.

12. City where an earthquake got Paul out of prison.

13. Athenians sneered at Paul's mention of this great event.

15. Paul saw this inscription: "To an unknown ____."

17. Elymas became this because of his deceit.

18. This missionary and Saul returned to Jerusalem.

21. Paul and Barnabas did signs and this in Iconium.

22. Where Paul was invited to preach in Pisidian Antioch.

Down

1. Girl who recognized Peter after he escaped prison.

2. How the Jerusalem council communicated with Gentiles of Antioch.

3. Man Cornelius was sent to get from Joppa.

5. Some in Judea said Gentiles must be ____ to be saved.

7. After Barnabas, Paul's next missionary partner.

9. Where Christians were first called by that title.

13. Where Peter went to pray.

14. Paul found Athens to be a city full of these.

16. Job of Cornelius.

17. After people were saved, they were this.

19. Cornelius saw one of these beings.

20. Greek God's name the people in Lystra called Barnabas.

CHOOSE THE BIBLE BOOK

Choose the correct answer.

1. The book that tells of Deborah's defeat of Sisera's army.
   - a. Joshua
   - b. Judges
   - c. 1 Samuel
   - d. 2 Chronicles

2. Book that uses the term guardian-redeemer nine times.
   - a. Esther
   - b. Joshua
   - c. Ruth
   - d. 1 Kings

3. This book records two censuses of the Israelites in the wilderness.
   - a. Exodus
   - b. Numbers
   - c. Deuteronomy
   - d. Leviticus

4. In his book, this minor prophet addressed God in prayer—not the people as is normal in books of prophecy.
   - a. Amos
   - b. Obadiah
   - c. Micah
   - d. Habakkuk

5. This New Testament gospel contains the most parables.
   - a. Matthew
   - b. Mark
   - c. Luke
   - d. John

6. For which New Testament book do scholars have no consensus on who wrote it?
   a. Hebrews
   b. Revelation
   c. Acts
   d. Philemon

7. In this epistle, the author refers to Jesus's Sermon on the Mount at least thirty times.
   a. Colossians
   b. James
   c. Ephesians
   d. 2 Timothy

8. The Old Testament book that is most often quoted in the New Testament.
   a. Isaiah
   b. Psalms
   c. Genesis
   d. Exodus

9. In what Old Testament book does the word *meaningless* occur thirty-three times (NIV)?
   a. Job
   b. Lamentations
   c. Jeremiah
   d. Ecclesiastes

10. In what book is the author told to draw the city of Jerusalem on a clay tablet?
    a. Jeremiah
    b. Ezekiel
    c. Daniel
    d. Isaiah

—— *Answer key on page 139.* ——

PARABLES CROSSWORD

*"So was fulfilled what was spoken through the prophet:
'I will open my mouth in parables.'" —Matthew 13:35*

Across

4. In the parable of the minas, the good investors got to be in charge of these.

5. In the Good Samaritan story, the traveler was going to this city.

8. Jesus said the "kingdom of heaven is like . . . fine ____."

10. In the parable of the net, a fisherman throws out the ____ fish.

12. The shepherd who found the one lost sheep put him here.

14. Tribal identity of the second man in the Good Samaritan story who passed by.

17. Response of the older brother about the party thrown for the prodigal son.

19. The kingdom of heaven is like a hidden ____.

21. The kingdom of heaven is like this seed.

22. Forgive seventy-seven times not just this many times.

23. Who the widow kept begging for help.

Down

1. In the wedding banquet parable, Jesus said, "Many are invited, but few are ____."

2. The prodigal son tended these animals.

3. The Pharisee and the tax collector both did this—though differently.

4. The Good Samaritan gave the innkeeper two of these.

6. Occupation of the first man in the Good Samaritan story who passed the injured man.

7. "Heaven and earth will pass away," but Jesus's ____ stand forever.

8. Early and late vineyard workers both got the same ____.

9. Jesus said people don't put new ____ in old skins.

11. In the ten virgins parable, Jesus said, "You do not know the day or the ____."

13. Jesus said, "Where your treasure is, there will your ____ be also."

15. In the parable of the wedding feast, Jesus said the humble would be this.

16. These ate the seeds the farmer sowed.

18. Jesus said no one sews a patch on an old ____.

20. What the foolish man built his house on.

GATES IN THE BIBLE
WORD SEARCH

Words may be horizontal, vertical, or diagonal, forward or backward, and may overlap.

```
W  A  T  E  R  B  N  A  U  T  W  M  M  X  V
Y  J  R  H  S  Y  P  A  T  R  Z  J  V  V  E
I  F  E  W  B  E  T  H  L  E  H  E  M  X  P
G  N  O  R  D  V  H  O  D  F  F  I  S  H  H
J  K  S  U  I  S  R  P  R  U  N  X  Q  C  R
E  E  W  P  N  C  S  H  A  L  E  M  H  G  A
Z  Z  R  L  E  T  H  P  S  Y  V  A  H  V  I
Y  Q  G  U  U  C  A  O  N  V  E  G  S  Y  M
B  Y  X  A  S  F  T  I  B  T  H  L  N  T  E
P  E  R  S  I  A  I  I  N  K  O  I  L  U  H
W  G  A  Z  A  R  L  T  O  V  R  M  B  A  D
S  H  E  E  P  F  A  E  U  N  S  H  Z  E  V
B  T  J  Z  Y  C  P  M  M  A  E  L  T  E  M
S  O  D  O  M  H  B  D  A  M  E  K  A  A  Y
F  F  E  E  S  P  H  Z  L  S  H  B  P  H  G
```

BEATIFUL	FISH	INSPECTION	SHALEM
BETHLEHEM	FOUNTAIN	JERICHO	SHEEP
DUNG	GATH	JERUSALEM	SODOM
EAST	GAZA	PERSIA	VALLEY
EPHRAIM	HORSE	SAMARIA	WATER

Answer key on page 140.

OLD TESTAMENT PRIESTS
WORD SEARCH

*Words may be horizontal, vertical, or diagonal,
forward or backward, and may overlap.*

```
E J A J S H E L E M I A H M Y
P L U B O A P H I N E H A S I
A F I S I S S K C U D D Z J T
S S Z A Q H H G U I A X T E H
H Z A Y S R U U Y Z A W A H A
H Z O J E H O R A M M A H O M
U Z H E N A I I C M A Z I I A
R A U O B A M B V P Z A M A R
O D U R P O A A K W I R E D J
J O J C I H E R R F A I L A N
Q K E M G A N Z O I H A E I A
Y E L I P U H I R N A H K D D
M I S X P R E F M A Z H H R A
E L E A Z A R T J R W J M Q B
F G H I L K I A H B I Y C T I
```

AARON   ELEAZAR   ITHAMAR   PHINEHAS
ABIHU   ELI   JEHOIADA   SHELEMIAH
AHIMELEK   ELIASHIB   JEHORAM   URIAH
AMARIAH   EZRA   JOSHUA   ZADOK
AMAZIAH   HILKIAH   NADAB
AZARIAH   HOPHNI   PASHHUR

SALVATION TERMS
WORD SEARCH

*Words may be horizontal, vertical, or diagonal,
forward or backward, and may overlap.*

```
S  P  Z  I  M  P  U  T  A  T  I  O  N  R  R  E
W  R  R  R  D  I  E  C  C  R  N  H  X  E  E  F
O  E  M  E  E  C  O  L  V  I  X  G  B  M  P  O
A  D  E  U  D  B  O  W  E  H  H  P  P  I  E  R
D  E  C  W  G  E  I  N  H  C  Y  A  C  S  N  E
O  M  V  F  R  B  S  R  F  F  T  M  V  S  T  K
P  P  I  D  A  P  W  T  T  E  D  I  Y  I  A  N
T  T  X  H  C  I  O  O  I  H  S  G  O  O  N  O
I  I  Y  P  E  Y  T  H  S  N  T  S  J  N  C  W
O  O  G  G  L  C  U  H  V  V  A  R  I  Z  E  L
N  N  H  R  E  G  E  N  E  R  A  T  I  O  N  E
C  R  E  C  O  N  C  I  L  I  A  T  I  O  N  D
N  L  A  T  O  N  E  M  E  N  T  Q  L  O  G  G
U  J  U  S  T  I  F  I  C  A  T  I  O  N  N  E
C  R  I  G  H  T  E  O  U  S  N  E  S  S  J  A
U  T  R  U  S  T  E  N  Q  B  E  L  I  E  F  R
```

ADOPTION   GRACE   RECONCILIATION
ATONEMENT   IMPUTATION   REDEMPTION
BELIEF   JUSTIFICATION   REGENERATION
CONFESSION   PREDESTINATION   REMISSION
ELECTION   REBIRTH   REPENTANCE
FAITH   RIGHTEOUSNESS
FOREKNOWLEDGE   TRUST

AVOID THESE THINGS

Fill in the blanks.

1. "Reject every kind of _____"
   (1 Thessalonians 5:22).

2. "Watch out for those who cause _____"
   (Romans 16:17).

3. "Avoid foolish _____ . . . about the law"
   (Titus 3:9).

4. "Do not _____ to the pattern of this world"
   (Romans 12:2).

5. "Bad _____ corrupts good character"
   (1 Corinthians 15:33).

6. "Do not be _____ together with unbeliev-
   ers" (2 Corinthians 6:14).

7. "Do everything without _____ or arguing"
   (Philippians 2:14).

8. "Do not give the _____ a foothold"
   (Ephesians 4:27).

9. "Do not store up for yourselves _____ on
   earth" (Matthew 6:19).

10. "Let us consider how we may spur one another on
    toward love and good deeds, not giving up
    _____ together" (Hebrews 10:24–25).

11. "Do not _____ the Spirit" (1 Thessalonians 5:19).

12. "Let no _____ communication proceed out
    of your mouth" (Ephesians 4:29 KJV).

—— Answer key on page 141. ——

BIBLE PEOPLE WHO CRIED
WORD SEARCH

Words may be horizontal, vertical, or diagonal,
forward or backward, and may overlap.

```
H Z Y F M W E E P N K E X T C
E E H I D A V I D E S A U I Y
L Z Z N U Z J N J W T U G M P
I Q I E A W D O B H L E M O J
S H S J K O Q C N Q A V R T O
H A N S E I M R E A S N U H S
A G H E N R A I Z A T U N Y E
C A I Y H A E H R L U H S A P
L R Z A M E I M A D E H A E H
Y Q E R C A M T I Q Q I S N J
J N S I E E H I P A B T N O A
O H F E E H D A A Y H O C A J
B J O A S H T R R H G R C M D
G K S F C O K S O B X E Q A H
P A U L D G M I E M A Y L G J
```

ABRAHAM	EZRA	JOASH	NAOMI
DANIEL	HANNAH	JOB	NEHEMIAH
DAVID	HAGAR	JONATHAN	PAUL
ELISHA	HEZEKIAH	JOSEPH	PETER
EGYPTIANS	JACOB	JOSHUA	TIMOTHY
ESAU	JEREMIAH	MORDECAI	
ESTHER	JESUS	MOSES	

BIBLICAL CANON STUDIES
WORD SEARCH

*Words may be horizontal, vertical, or diagonal,
forward or backward, and may overlap.*

```
M C R K A U T O G R A P H S P
M W A S H S Y V B H C H N V Y
A A Y N E H C T B X Q G E A U
N P L G O P N R I B C C W T T
U L P E D N T U I R V N Q I O
S E U Y X K I U S B O Z D C Q
C N R D M A Y C A U E H N A V
R A J A C V N C I G R S T N G
I R K M O R V D N T I Y H U H
P Y Y N D Z X Y R A Y N P S A
T X J V E R B A L I R L T A U
F N N Q X R H X F Q A R L D P
Z A P O C R Y P H A H N E B E
W R I N S P I R A T I O N N R
D S W R Q A S C R O L L S W I
```

ALEXANDRIAN
APOCRYPHA
AUTHORITY
AUTOGRAPHS
CANONICITY
CODEX

INSPIRATION
INERRANCY
MANUSCRIPT
PAPYRUS
PLENARY
SEPTUAGINT

SCRIBES
SCROLLS
VATICANUS
VERBAL

PICK THE BIBLE BOOKS

Pick the Bible book that best fits the description.

1. Old Testament book telling of several unusual visions.
   - a. Job
   - b. Ezekiel
   - c. Habakkuk
   - d. Ecclesiastes

2. This Old Testament book has the most words of any book of the Bible.
   - a. Jeremiah
   - b. Psalms
   - c. Isaiah
   - d. 2 Chronicles

3. In this New Testament book, the author mentions that he wrote his epistle in very large letters.
   - a. Galatians
   - b. Ephesians
   - c. Philippians
   - d. Colossians

4. The New Testament book written to a young pastor on Crete.
   - a. 1 Timothy
   - b. Titus
   - c. 2 Thessalonians
   - d. Philemon

5. This Old Testament book is about a reluctant evangelist who was successful but unhappy.
   - a. Ezra
   - b. Jeremiah
   - c. Daniel
   - d. Jonah

6. This Old Testament book tells about a queen from Sheba who visits Solomon.
    a. 2 Samuel
    b. 2 Chronicles
    c. 2 Kings
    d. Nehemiah

7. These two Old Testament books do not mention God.
    a. Ruth and Esther
    b. Ecclesiastes and Song of Songs
    c. Esther and Song of Songs
    d. Ruth and Song of Songs

8. These two New Testament books have a genealogy of Jesus.
    a. Matthew and Mark
    b. Mark and Luke
    c. Matthew and Luke
    d. Matthew and John

9. This New Testament book demonstrates the contrast between the Old Testament tabernacle and the one true tabernacle, Jesus.
    a. Hebrews
    b. 1 Corinthians
    c. James
    d. Acts

10. This New Testament book records a number of Old Testament era people who were faithful.
    a. Romans
    b. Revelation
    c. John
    d. Hebrews

SCHEMES AND PLOTS CROSSWORD

"As they plot their crimes, they say, 'We have devised the perfect plan!' Yes, the human heart and mind are cunning." —Psalm 64:6 NLT

Across

2. Jacob and Rachel tricked him.

4. This man plotted to kill his brother out of jealousy.

5. In Thessalonica, a group plotted to seize this missionary, but failed.

7. Herodias schemed to have this man beheaded.

9. This woman tricked her father-in-law, Judah.

10. He connived to lead soldiers to Jesus.

14. He plotted against Job.

15. This queen schemed to steal Naboth's vineyard.

16. This son of King David tried to overthrow him.

17. His wife schemed against Joseph.

19. He came up with a plan to make sure baby Jesus was killed.

Down

1. He tried to arrange for all Persian Jews to be killed.

3. He tried to disrupt Nehemiah's wall-rebuilding plans.

5. These religious leaders plotted to kill Jesus.

6. The chief priests plotted to kill this friend of Jesus, whom He had raised from the dead.

8. Synagogue leaders silenced this New Testament saint by stoning him.

11. Some Chaldeans railroaded this godly man about prayer.

12. Replaced by King David, this man was the first king of Israel.

13. She connived against Samson.

18. This brother saved Joseph from their other brothers' schemes.

THE PEOPLE IN LUKE
WORD SEARCH

*Words may be horizontal, vertical, or diagonal,
forward or backward, and may overlap.*

```
G A A Z E L I Z A B E T H U S
L S N U C F G D F N T U Z S I
P A I D G Z R J D N Q E E H M
I F Q M R U J U D A S L C P E
L Z J S O E S K L E V I H G O
A B I A F N W T Z C H J A M N
T O R L A Z A R U S I A R A T
E R W C V A N N A S T H I T U
T H E O P H I L U S G Q A T W
G A B R I E L D F A R G H H M
I J B S S H D P W R H I Q E X
Y Y L F E U J O H N Y T E W I
P E P A E S S E R G D R R D I
J O S E P H O E A E G X A A V
Q R Q F T I R M J I H R N M M
```

ANDREW	HEROD	LEVI	SIMEON
ANNA	JESUS	MARTHA	SIMON
AUGUSTUS	JOHN	MARY	THEOPHILUS
ELIJAH	JOSEPH	MATTHEW	ZECHARIAH
ELIZABETH	JUDAS	MOSES	
GABRIEL	LAZARUS	PILATE	

Answer key on page 143.

"B" MEN
WORD SEARCH

Words may be horizontal, vertical, or diagonal, forward or backward, and may overlap.

```
O  B  T  J  M  W  E  P  F  K  B  B  Y  F  Z
B  C  A  V  B  E  S  A  I  B  A  A  H  V  B
A  N  P  L  P  K  B  R  J  P  R  K  B  Y  E
F  B  E  D  A  N  D  B  H  B  A  B  E  X  L
M  A  J  B  I  A  O  U  Z  O  K  A  Z  D  S
L  R  J  O  J  Z  M  Q  H  A  H  K  A  B  H
B  T  J  A  E  I  K  S  U  Z  G  K  L  I  A
E  I  B  N  S  X  R  N  A  H  D  A  E  L  Z
N  M  K  E  J  A  R  E  I  B  C  R  L  D  Z
O  A  G  R  T  R  B  T  J  M  B  U  L  A  A
D  E  T  G  X  H  R  A  S  R  A  A  R  D  R
W  U  T  E  P  D  U  E  N  W  E  J  R  A  N
G  S  P  S  Z  R  A  E  K  R  Q  Z  N  A  B
O  B  E  R  E  D  B  L  L  E  A  B  E  E  B
B  E  R  A  K  A  H  H  N  B  B  B  X  B  B
```

BAKBAKKAR	BARUCH	BERAKAH	BILDAD
BALAAM	BEKER	BERED	BOANERGES
BARABBAS	BEDAN	BESAI	BOAZ
BARAK	BELSHAZZAR	BETHUEL	
BARNABAS	BENJAMIN	BEZALEL	
BARTIMAEUS	BENO	BEZER	

REVELATION 1–3 CROSSWORD

"Whoever has ears, let them hear what the Spirit says to the churches." —Revelation 2:7

Across

2. God sent one of these to John.

3. Jesus said, "I am the Alpha and the _____."

6. What Jesus told the first church to do.

7. The second church Jesus addressed.

9. Jesus said, "I am the first and the _____."

11. Blessing goes to the one who reads the words of this.

12. John saw one with this color hair.

13. First church addressed.

Down

1. Jesus said, "Whoever has ears, let them _____."

4. Those who overcame were promised this.

5. What John was "in" on the Lord's Day.

8. The lampstands represented these.

9. John saw seven of these.

10. Number of churches that were addressed.

BOOK OF HEBREWS CROSSWORD

What do you know about the book of Hebrews?

Across

4. Old Testament man who did not see death.

5. By faith this city's walls fell.

6. Entertain these, who might be angels.

7. Jesus said, "Radiance of God's _____."

9. Believers are told "Do not harden your _____."

10. God's Word is sharper than a two-edged _____.

12. Jesus was sacrificed "once for _____."

14. Melchizedek was king of this.

15. Jesus is the believers' high _____.

19. Times a year the priest entered the Most Holy Place.

21. People are destined to die and face this.

22. Abraham lived in these in the Promised Land.

Down

1. Approach the throne of grace with this.

2. He was an Old Testament high priest.

3. We should not give up "_____ together."

5. We should fix "our eyes on _____."

8. What the old covenant had become.

11. The Hebrews were called "slow to _____."

13. "In these _____ days he has spoken to us by his Son."

16. Jesus is seated at the _____ hand of God.

17. The author did not have this to tell about Gideon and others.

18. Jesus is "superior to _____."

20. People of faith long for a better _____.

NEW TESTAMENT CITIES AND TOWNS
WORD SEARCH

*Words may be horizontal, vertical, or diagonal,
forward or backward, and may overlap.*

```
M A Q Y D A M A S C U S K B J
X I N E E W L S N A I N Z D B
S W L T G B C Y D E R B E K W
L M T E I A E U S S R J L Z S
R Y Y L T O H R S T E O S L L
I C D R L U C P E Y R L M X Y
L P O D N T S H H A C A A E M
L Q E L A A A I M T G H D A A
C S M R O F E R A U E L A J G
J Y U M G S S R S M I B W R A
S S R S N A S N A U E N J B D
F C N E E A M A E S S L O Z A
O U X Y N H R U E H E Q O C N
D P I V M E P Y M W T A Z T I
M G B A B B Q E M X E A C A P
```

ANTIOCH	CYRENE	LYSTRA	PTOLEMAIS
ATHENS	DAMASCUS	MAGADAN	ROME
BETHPHAGE	DERBE	MILETUS	SELA
BEREA	EPHESUS	MYRA	SMYRNA
CAESAREA	ICONIUM	NAIN	SYCHAR
COLOSSAE	LYDDA	PERGAMUM	TARSUS

—— Answer key on page 145. ——

BIBLE WRITERS
WORD SEARCH

*Words may be horizontal, vertical, or diagonal,
forward or backward, and may overlap.*

```
E  L  J  J  S  G  J  X  M  R  F  C  J  D  V
C  U  N  J  U  T  J  A  S  A  P  H  O  F  Z
J  K  A  P  O  R  N  J  R  X  R  N  N  R  P
Q  E  H  M  R  S  K  H  J  F  J  K  A  F  J
P  X  U  T  O  U  H  N  O  Y  P  U  H  R  O
X  E  M  T  L  S  G  U  A  J  N  Q  D  J  E
G  N  T  K  V  E  E  A  A  H  J  A  N  E  L
E  T  W  E  V  H  O  S  E  A  T  L  H  B  G
Z  F  B  G  R  P  M  D  E  T  H  A  U  T  T
E  I  S  A  I  A  H  G  D  L  D  K  N  A  E
K  D  A  N  I  E  L  X  V  Z  G  I  C  N  P
I  C  S  O  Z  B  S  H  V  S  X  A  V  O  M
E  R  I  O  B  A  D  I  A  H  C  F  R  A  G
L  J  H  S  D  R  M  A  T  T  H  E  W  Z  D
A  M  O  S  B  J  H  F  H  A  G  G  A  I  E
```

AGUR	EZRA	JOSHUA	NATHAN
AMOS	HAGGAI	JUDE	OBADIAH
ASAPH	HOSEA	LUKE	PAUL
DANIEL	ISAIAH	MARK	PETER
DAVID	JOEL	MATTHEW	
ETHAN	JOHN	MOSES	
EZEKIEL	JONAH	NAHUM	

—— Answer key on page 146. ——

EZRA AND NEHEMIAH CROSSWORD

"The God of heaven will make us prosper, and we his servants will arise and build." —Nehemiah 2:20 ESV

Across

1. The first gate rebuilt in Jerusalem.

4. This king searched for the decree of an earlier king.

8. What Nehemiah rode to examine the damage.

10. King's decree in Ezra 1 said to build this.

11. Wall-builders had to have a tool in one hand and this in the other.

13. This wood for the temple came from Lebanon.

14. Artaxerxes gave a letter to Ezra saying the Jews could go back to this land.

16. Laying the foundation, the people said of God, "His love . . . endures ____."

19. Those opposing the temple sent this to Artaxerxes.

20. First thing built by returning Jews.

21. Nehemiah was in the citadel of this town.

Down

2. Darius let the wall rebuilding resume, and he ____ for it.

3. Days it took to rebuild the wall.

5. Tobiah said this animal could knock down the wall.

6. Artaxerxes told the Jews to do this at the temple site.

7. A problem in Jerusalem was that men had married ____ women.

9. Neighbors gave returning Jews gold and this.

11. Nehemiah's brother told him this had fallen in Jerusalem.

12. After the temple had been built, the Jews celebrated this special day.

13. King of Persia in Ezra 1.

15. Older priests did this upon seeing the new temple's foundation.

17. This teacher came to Jerusalem from Babylon.

18. Two minor prophets, Zechariah and this man, prophesied to the Jews during this time.

19. What Ezra read to the people after the wall was built.

BIBLE SUPERLATIVES CROSSWORD

"They kept quiet because on the way they had argued about who was the greatest." —Mark 9:34

Across

4. Most outspoken disciple.

5. Tallest man.

7. Strongest man.

9. Most persecuted man.

10. Most sorrowful prophet.

11. Most disloyal friend.

12. Most doubtful disciple.

Down

1. Most beautiful queen.

2. Most well-traveled missionary.

3. Oldest man.

6. Worst king.

7. Richest man.

8. Most humble man of his time.

10. Longest engagement.

1 SAMUEL CROSSWORD

"People look at the outward appearance, but the LORD looks at the heart." —1 Samuel 16:7

Across

3. Samuel anointed him to be the first king.
5. Hophni and Phineas's jobs.
7. Hannah made her son one of these each year.
8. David's father.
9. Samuel thought Eli called him; it was really _____.
10. Samuel becomes a _____ over Israel.
13. Hannah's husband.
14. When Hannah prayed, Eli thought she was this.
16. Goliath asked David, "Am I a _____?"
17. She provoked Hannah.
19. The Philistines captured this valuable item from Israel.
20. Samuel told the Israelites to get rid of these foreign things.
22. What Israel wanted to have as their leader.
23. Goliath's hometown.

Down

1. Hannah's baby boy.
2. 1 Samuel 2:12 says Eli's sons were this.
3. Object Samuel named Ebenezer.
4. Afraid, Saul hid among this.
6. The first king was from this tribe.
8. Saul's son.
11. Hophni and Phineas's dad.
12. Where Hannah and her husband worshiped.
15. When Eli heard bad news about his sons and the ark, he fell and broke this.
16. When Saul failed, Samuel anointed this man as the next king.
18. Samuel grew in stature and _____ with the Lord and with people.
21. The weapon David used against Goliath.

—— Answer key on page 147. ——

WORD SEARCH
& ACTIVITY BOOK

SOLUTIONS

AND

ANSWERS

Lesser-Known Women Word Search

```
R P C N Q F Y R T Y V Q C S R V
O E E E A T F S A Y X V O H A L
V N R X S A D O M R Q G F V H O
Z I T S L P M H A Z S X D N I I
I N A P C W S A R I I P S T N S
J N Z B R F J E H K U B Y F O Y
M A T E I R I W K Q Q N N P A Z
U H D A Z G N A S E N A T H M E
L T H J L C A N D A C E Y C B G
Y U E F O R A I S R S B C X I L
V A A K S A H T L V T J H W L A
P E R S I S N U P F M G E D H H
E L H R C Y V N F G J K P K A E
H I S A L O M E A O X P J U H O
J X S S U S A N N A R N E M V G
C O R P A H E S V A S H T I L K
```

Lands of the Bible

1. Ephesus
2. Bethsaida
3. Jerusalem
4. Caesarea
5. Beersheba
6. Joppa
7. Caesarea Philippi
8. Bethlehem
9. Laodicea
10. Capernaum

Paul Said It in 1 Corinthians

1. foolishness
2. crucified
3. temple
4. truth
5. love
6. death
7. childish
8. grow
9. Lord
10. baptize

The People of Matthew's Genealogy Word Search

```
T  B  I  B  W  C  X  J  O  S  I  A  H  P  P  P  U
A  B  R  A  H  A  M  U  R  U  E  A  G  E  V  F  U
M  U  P  S  A  R  J  E  B  T  F  S  A  R  L  H  E
A  S  U  J  O  P  W  J  C  Q  M  Y  W  E  O  N  W
T  O  A  Z  H  L  F  D  K  X  A  F  E  Z  M  Q  H
T  Y  B  M  Z  R  O  F  B  A  N  V  T  Y  O  W  E
H  Y  C  E  M  I  G  M  G  A  A  F  C  A  B  J  E
A  P  X  F  D  I  A  T  O  X  S  S  D  I  V  O  J
N  G  X  F  N  D  N  H  Z  N  S  N  E  J  L  S  U
Y  T  W  Q  Q  Y  O  A  R  T  E  N  N  H  E  E  D
W  N  J  J  U  V  O  R  D  Q  H  X  X  I  B  P  A
H  E  Z  E  K  I  A  H  S  A  L  M  O  N  U  H  H
D  R  W  S  J  W  K  K  X  J  B  G  J  X  D  E  N
L  W  W  S  R  P  O  Z  C  L  L  B  O  A  Z  L  P
X  Q  V  E  F  I  I  V  J  P  T  O  F  Q  D  E  V
L  J  A  C  O  B  Q  V  E  L  E  A  Z  A  R  W  H
P  D  A  V  I  D  O  Z  S  C  I  S  A  A  C  G  X
```

Proverbs 1–4 Word Search

```
P  V  D  P  U  T  X  H  U  M  B  L  E  K  F
D  I  S  C  E  R  N  I  N  G  I  J  C  Q  A
A  C  Z  B  K  V  H  T  L  D  B  W  P  U  I
D  O  P  L  P  R  D  T  C  O  W  B  R  B  T
D  M  R  E  R  K  I  W  L  U  V  T  E  L  H
T  M  U  S  O  G  N  G  U  A  N  E  C  A  F
E  A  D  S  S  R  H  O  H  M  E  E  I  M  U
A  N  E  E  P  A  T  G  W  T  L  H  O  E  L
C  D  N  D  E  C  M  N  N  L  E  A  U  L  N
H  S  T  F  R  E  T  O  A  O  E  O  S  E  E
I  U  P  R  I  G  H  T  D  S  M  D  U  S  S
N  T  D  Z  T  R  W  B  D  S  A  O  G  S  S
G  W  E  Q  Y  N  M  W  Y  Z  I  E  L  E  K
U  K  X  Q  H  O  N  O  R  D  P  W  L  O  P
A  D  I  S  C  R  E  T  I  O  N  C  N  P  S
```

Creation Story Fill-In

1. formless, empty
2. light, darkness
3. sky
4. dry, ground
5. land, seas
6. fruit, kinds
7. day, night
8. fruitful, number

PEOPLE GROUPS WORD SEARCH

```
I B H R V R A M O R I T E S O W
A E A E N H J X Y H H A W Q F A
Z A D B B A U A J N I M X G P P
Y G S O Y R P Z V L T M G R A I
E V G S M L E C R Q T O P E O S
G G O F Y I O W U A I N T E W R
N O Y M P R T N S X T I G K S A
I W Z P O I E I X E T A S O E
Z M M Z T A Z A S A S E L B J L
I I L Z J I B J N H N S I F U I
R O M A N S A I S S A S L P D T
J Y Z J S X Z N T R N F E A E E
Q M M X Q E M J S E B I A D A S
Z S A M A R I T A N S L N C N R
P H I L I S T I N E S C S Q S L
B P E R S I A N S M O F X C N L
```

SHAKESPEARE OR THE BIBLE?

1. b
2. b
3. a
4. b
5. a
6. b
7. a
8. b
9. b
10. a

HEALINGS BY JESUS

1. centurion
2. Peter
3. Jairus
4. Bartimaeus
5. Malchus, servant of the high priest
6. woman with twelve-year illness
7. leprosy
8. hand
9. widow
10. a pool of water

COMMON NOUNS IN GENESIS WORD SEARCH

SOLOMON'S TEMPLE WORD SEARCH

JESUS QUOTE FILL-IN

1. abolish, fulfill
2. mother
3. two
4. masters
5. wise, rock
6. test
7. repent
8. born again
9. thirst
10. believe

NAMES OF GOD WORD SEARCH

```
D A Y S P R I N G P O C A O A
E D A Y S T A R L L G O D G L
B L P P K I N G P U Z R O C P
R O O E U U L Y R T A N N R H
I C J R A X O S X R D E A E A
D O Y E D B G J G U V R I A I
E M Q A H K O B B T O S M T M
G F B U H O S Q R H C T A O M
R O H N S W V X P A A O J R A
O R A C L J E A R G T N E D N
O T U B B A K H H H E E S P U
M E K B B S A L M I G H T Y E
Y R Z I F A T H E R T B Y K L
X D E L I V E R E R Z K B P H
K S R A R E D E E M E R M X R
```

ANIMAL TERMS IN JOB 39 WORD SEARCH

```
M F F U R R O W D T F N T Y B
K F B Y K W K Z D F L G V U I
F S D E J I M X O D M O U N R
R E H Z Z N J O N V Y A F A T
P F A A B G J I K I A T A H H
Q I Z T W S X Y E E D S W O D
Z K N D H K A X Y X G H N R C
Y O P I J E H A D O E G B S N
H N A B O P R M S C O Y S E E
Y E W K U N Y S X Q R M E O S
N W S F X O S R V O J S A E T
Z J P H A R N E S S N O G Q W
O S T R I C H D T G C A L T S
J A V Z S T O R K T C R E U H
M F L I G H T M A N E B Q W A
```

WHICH IS IT? ELISHA, ELIJAH, OR BOTH?

1. Elijah
2. Both
3. Elijah
4. Elijah
5. Elijah
6. Elijah
7. Elijah
8. Elisha
9. Elijah
10. Elijah
11. Elisha
12. Elisha
13. Both

FLYING CREATURES IN THE BIBLE WORD SEARCH

BIBLE FOOD AND DRINK CROSSWORD

PSALM 19 WORD SEARCH

I'VE JUST SEEN JESUS:
POST-RESURRECTION APPEARANCES

1. Mary Magdalene
2. John
3. Peter
4. a ghost
5. Emmaus
6. Thomas
7. hands and side
8. breakfast
9. 500
10. Mount of Olives

MIRACLES IN THE WILDERNESS

1. Red Sea
2. Aaron
3. wind
4. Sinai
5. bronze
6. cloud
7. fire
8. leprosy
9. Egyptian
10. wood
11. speak to it
12. Korah

CHARACTERISTICS OF THE GODLY WORD SEARCH

MOSES CROSSWORD

THE ARK OF THE COVENANT

1. mercy seat
2. rectangular
3. with poles
4. Uzzah
5. tabernacle
6. temple
7. Philistines
8. plague
9. Aaron's rod that budded, the Ten Commandments, manna
10. cherubim
11. David
12. blood of a sacrificed animal

MONEY BIBLE VERSES

1. G
2. C
3. I
4. L
5. D
6. E
7. F
8. K
9. A
10. B
11. H
12. J

PROPHECIES ABOUT JESUS CROSSWORD

"A" MEN

1. Aaron	4. Agrippa	7. Asaph	10. Amos
2. Abednego	5. Andrew	8. Abel	11. Ananias
3. Absalom	6. Aquila	9. Adam	12. Asher

WHERE DOES THIS BOOK BELONG?

1. A	4. B	7. D	10. C
2. E	5. C	8. A	11. A
3. D	6. E	9. D	12. C

APOSTLE PAUL CROSSWORD

GOD'S ATTRIBUTES WORD SEARCH

WHAT THE HOLY SPIRIT DOES WORD SEARCH

SPELL CHECK

1. c	5. b	9. b
2. b.	6. a	10. c
3. a	7. c	11. a
4. b	8. c	12. c

WORDS FROM REVELATION SCRAMBLE

1. prophecy
2. church
3. seven
4. hallelujah
5. worthy
6. lamb
7. angels
8. vision
9. revelation
10. lukewarm
11. tribulation
12. throne
13. elders
14. scroll
15. seals
16. trumpets
17. judgment
18. beast
19. heaven
20. earth

MATTHEW 1–14 CROSSWORD

HE MARRIED WHOM? CROSSWORD

COMMANDS FROM GOD

1. G	3. G	5. F	7. H	9. E
2. A	4. B	6. D	8. C	10. F

JUST ONE BOOK

1. N	6. G	11. E	16. F
2. C	7. O	12. K	17. L
3. B	8. R	13. P	18. J
4. I	9. H	14. A	
5. Q	10. M	15. D	

OLD TESTAMENT TOWNS AND CITIES WORD SEARCH

LEVITICUS WORD SEARCH

MICHAEL OR GABRIEL?

1. Michael
2. Gabriel
3. Gabriel
4. Michael
5. Michael
6. Michael
7. Gabriel
8. Gabriel

BOOKS OF THE BIBLE SCRAMBLE

1. Habakkuk
2. Philemon
3. Matthew
4. Chronicles
5. Exodus
6. Jeremiah
7. Revelation
8. Thessalonians
9. Haggai
10. Lamentations
11. Timothy
12. Corinthians
13. Deuteronomy
14. Nehemiah
15. Philippians
16. Obadiah
17. Malachi
18. Ephesians
19. Leviticus
20. Hebrews

GOD IS . . . WORD SEARCH

JOB 39 WORD SEARCH

PSALMS CROSSWORD

WHAT TO WEAR

1. Jesus
2. Old Testament Jewish priests
3. Martyred saints (Revelation 6:11)
4. Joseph (son of Jacob)
5. John the Baptist
6. Adam and Eve
7. King Saul
8. Samuel
9. Paul
10. King David

NOAH AND THE ARK WORD SEARCH

GENESIS CROSSWORD

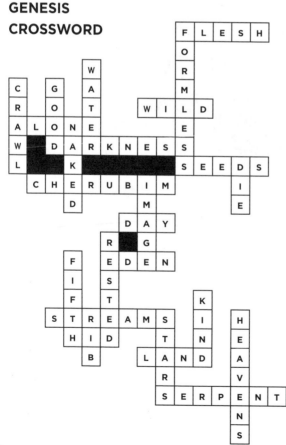

BATTLE GEAR WORD SEARCH

```
L  J  W  W  C  H  H  S  X  A  G  O  L  A  J
E  I  S  I  C  K  L  E  H  S  W  O  R  D  M
W  F  F  Q  E  C  W  V  L  I  G  T  S  M  A
P  E  Q  S  F  F  H  K  Y  M  E  D  Q  N  T
E  R  A  X  X  R  A  A  T  L  E  L  Y  S  T
J  P  T  P  R  X  J  S  R  J  F  T  D  P  O
U  X  F  W  O  J  R  F  H  I  Z  U  Y  E  C
Z  P  G  U  I  N  I  Z  H  E  O  F  A  A  K
F  X  B  R  E  A  S  T  P  L  A  T  E  R  B
O  H  P  L  D  A  R  M  O  R  J  T  V  F  O
Q  A  R  R  O  W  C  U  V  X  R  U  H  G  W
J  Z  M  M  I  A  E  E  H  O  R  S  E  N  H
D  J  A  V  E  L  I  N  M  F  D  Y  A  U  E
M  L  A  X  E  S  K  W  H  G  V  I  Y  L  T
I  N  C  H  A  I  N  M  A  I  L  J  X  G  O
```

ALTAR BUILDERS WORD SEARCH

```
A  X  J  T  Y  Y  S  W  W  N  T  W  D  I  A
C  H  F  O  N  E  L  I  J  A  H  P  W  B  B
I  Q  A  O  S  I  R  U  T  M  Q  Z  Y  J  R
B  S  D  B  B  H  M  H  N  G  O  E  I  I  A
J  L  A  W  T  A  U  O  Z  I  R  R  G  V  H
N  A  C  A  H  Z  L  A  S  K  F  U  R  J  A
U  C  P  C  F  M  A  B  E  M  B  S  E  J  M
G  H  R  O  M  Q  Z  D  K  B  S  B  V  R  A
I  B  Q  I  B  I  Q  G  Y  M  M  A  K  O  W
D  M  A  N  A  S  S  E  H  A  W  B  I  B  S
E  V  W  Z  M  H  J  B  P  N  V  E  O  O  A
O  D  M  M  W  G  J  L  L  O  I  L  G  A  T
N  N  M  Z  S  A  U  L  A  A  R  O  G  M  I
I  I  X  N  O  A  H  A  S  H  H  C  W  X  I
N  S  A  M  U  E  L  L  D  A  V  I  D  B  C
```

EVENTS IN JERUSALEM

1. David
2. Absalom
3. Solomon
4. Nebuchadnezzar
5. Cyrus
6. Nehemiah
7. Herod
8. Peter
9. Stephen
10. Jesus
11. Gethsemane
12. temple

EARLY CHURCHES WORD SEARCH

```
J L I C O N I U M L Y C M M E
J E P H E Y U G E Y G C R D C
P S R E F L M A R S N O Y E O
C H M U R M A Y Z T J R G R L
M A I Y S G T O A R K I A B O
R H N L R A A C D A C N L E S
V U F T A N L M R I C T A Y S
U T Z L I D A E U L C H T K A
R O M E Z O E Q M M E E I C E
T R O A S N C L O I I A A P I
R S A R D I S H P Y W E J Q I
J T H Y A T I R A H T D N Z X
R C K K Z W P H I L I P P I T
T H E S S A L O N I C A C F B
Y P T R Z E P H E S U S J C F
```

CALLED! CROSSWORD

SPIRITUAL GIFTS WORD SEARCH

WHAT GOD GIVES THE BELIEVER WORD SEARCH

LAST WORDS

1. David (1 Kings 2:9)
2. Joseph (Genesis 50:25)
3. Samson (Judges 16:28)
4. King Saul (1 Samuel 31:4)
5. Joshua (Joshua 24:27)
6. Daniel (Daniel 12:8)
7. Jesus (Acts 1:8)
8. Stephen (Acts 7:60)
9. Peter (2 Peter 3:18)
10. Moses (Deuteronomy 33:29)

NAMES OF JESUS WORD SEARCH

MORE NAMES OF JESUS WORD SEARCH

BIBLE MISSIONARIES, PASTORS, AND EVANGELISTS

1. Silas
2. John the Baptist
3. Noah
4. Paul
5. Jonah
6. Luke
7. Barnabas
8. Philip
9. Apollos
10. John Mark

PSALM VERSE FILL-IN CROSSWORD

PSALM 119 WORD SEARCH

WEIGHTS AND MEASURES WORD SEARCH

```
K N G P L H Y L L S G X H Y K
M O O V A D J Z E S P A E S F
C U B I T C A H Q R D A Q H S
C W I C A B E X H Z O H N E F
D O D F E K P R E E D A D K A
M D R E U A N J N K Q N B E T
U Y H I N R A U L D Y D E L H
F Z P C F E L W Z N Z B K N O
H U Q M I C H O N I Z R A W M
M I L E Q A E O N P K E H C B
T M A B W F P P M G Z A U Z L
Z H N M A N E H H E Y D O G G
D T A L W Q K N P A R T R A C
R B A T H V X G X B H H S I I
M E A S U R E W B O M E R K R
```

BIBLE MOUNTAINS WORD SEARCH

```
C C A R M E L C Q J A W A L A
G B Q S H G S Z O N T V B E R
E G X E J Z I H A R A B A B A
R Z U I A T P L E L C B R A R
I K Y R X A I H E P M D I N A
Z O E W G B S A P A H O M O T
I Z L P I O G L E T D E N N K
M F F I H R A A H B B H R O X
J F C H V R H K W E A S G Z B
Y O H O R E O I F I R L G I J
C M O M R Z S N I I A M E O L
V Y S L Y Q X N E B O R O N I
I A B S I N A I M I Z A R N D
T H H M O R I A H M K X B B T
Y X G I L B O A H O R E B I P
```

BIBLE-TIME PROFESSIONS WORD SCRAMBLE

1. mason (2 Kings 12:12)
2. painter (Jeremiah 22:14)
3. seamstress (Ezekiel 13:18)
4. brickmaker (Genesis 11:3)
5. tanner (Acts 9:43)
6. gardener (Jeremiah 29:5)
7. musician (2 Samuel 6:5)
8. coppersmith (2 Timothy 4:14)
9. silversmith (Acts 19:24)
10. tailor (Exodus 39:1)
11. butler (Genesis 40:2)
12. weaver (Exodus 28:32)
13. potter (Isaiah 64:8)
14. jeweler (Exodus 28:17-21)
15. spinner (Exodus 35:25)

MIRACLES HAPPEN CROSSWORD

POSITIVE COMMANDS IN SCRIPTURE

1. answer
2. patient
3. harmony
4. Spirit
5. content
6. anxiety
7. thanks
8. light
9. grace
10. confidence
11. armor
12. opportunity
13. sacrifice
14. self

BOOK OF ESTHER SEARCH

PLANTS OF THE BIBLE WORD SEARCH

BIBLE VERSE FILL-IN

1. knowledge
2. holy, holy
3. strong
4. warrior
5. sacrifice
6. humble
7. glory, work

8. gladness
9. compassions
10. rubies
11. harvest, workers
12. saved

ACTS 10–17 CROSSWORD

CHOOSE THE BIBLE BOOK

1. b
2. c
3. b
4. d
5. c
6. a
7. b
8. b
9. d
10. b

PARABLES CROSSWORD

GATES IN THE BIBLE WORD SEARCH

OLD TESTAMENT PRIESTS WORD SEARCH

SALVATION TERMS WORD SEARCH

AVOID THESE THINGS

1. evil
2. divisions
3. controversies
4. conform
5. company
6. yoked
7. grumbling
8. devil
9. treasures
10. meeting
11. quench
12. corrupt

BIBLE PEOPLE WHO CRIED WORD SEARCH

BIBLICAL CANON STUDIES WORD SEARCH

PICK THE BIBLE BOOKS

1. b
2. a
3. a
4. b
5. d
6. b
7. c
8. c
9. a
10. d

SCHEMES AND PLOTS CROSSWORD

THE PEOPLE IN LUKE WORD SEARCH

"B" MEN WORD SEARCH

REVELATION 1–3 CROSSWORD

144

BOOK OF HEBREWS CROSSWORD

NEW TESTAMENT CITIES AND TOWNS WORD SEARCH

BIBLE WRITERS WORD SEARCH

```
E L J J S G J X M R F C J D V
C U N J U T J A S A P H O F Z
J K A P O R N J R X R N R P
Q E H M R S K H J F K A F J
P X U T O U H N O Y P U H R O
X E M T L S G U A J N Q D J E
G N T K V E E A A H J A N E L
E T W E V H O S E A T L H B G
Z F B G R P M D E T H A U T T
E I S A I A H G D L D K N A E
K D A N I E L X V Z G I C N P
I C S O Z B S H V S X A V O M
E R I O B A D I A H C F R A G
L J H S D R M A T T H E W Z D
A M O S B J H F H A G G A I E
```

EZRA AND NEHEMIAH CROSSWORD

BIBLE SUPERLATIVES CROSSWORD

1 SAMUEL CROSSWORD